ESSAYS *That* WORKED®
for MEDICAL SCHOOLS

ESSAYS *That* WORKED®
for MEDICAL SCHOOLS

*40 Essays that Helped Students
Get Into the Nation's Top Medical Schools*

Edited by
STEPHANIE JONES
and EMILY ANGEL BAER

BALLANTINE BOOKS • NEW YORK

ACKNOWLEDGMENTS

We created this book with the help of many students, doctors, and admissions personnel at some of the top medical schools in America. We deeply appreciate the generosity of the applicants who let us reprint their essays and of the admissions officers who gave us their time, critiques, and advice.

We wish to extend our gratitude to several people in particular: Rollin Riggs, Nadine Cline, Dr. J. Harold Helderman, Nelson Strather, Dr. Bruce Alpert, Phil Kimrey, Tish W. Peterson, and Jodie Friedman. And for nonmedical support, thanks to Dennis Baer, Barry Ray, and Ellis Haguewood. All went far beyond their duties and gave us invaluable assistance.

CONTENTS

INTRODUCTION

Writing your personal statement on a medical school application is a big deal. But you've already figured that out; that's why you've got this book. Why is it a big deal? Because your essay is a blank slate upon which you intend to differentiate yourself from approximately 35,000 other smart people with the same desire to become a doctor.

It's true that the number of medical school applications has been declining recently. So your chance of landing one of the approximately 17,000 coveted positions in a med school class has improved to about 50 percent, assuming everyone is equal. But everyone isn't equal, or med schools would save themselves a lot of trouble and draw names out of a hat. Though right now you're probably thinking you'd be happy getting into *any* medical school, you'd rather have your pick of the best.

Once you get past the initial screening (often based solely on grades and Medical College Admissions Test [MCAT] scores), the personal statement is your opportunity to be noticed. Its relative importance does differ by school: More prominent schools tend to place more emphasis on the essay, if only because they receive more applications. The essay may not make much difference for an applicant who's an Olympic athlete, or one who holds a patent for a lifesaving device, but it does matter for the rest. The truth is, premedical students all look alike after you've read a few hundred applications.

More so than in law or business school admissions, the admissions officer is looking for signs that you are a compassionate, dedicated person who relates well to other people (i.e., patients). If you can't make this case for yourself on paper, they generally feel you won't be able to do it in person.

1

Applicants want to say the right thing. Unfortunately, the cliché "I want to help people" will make the reader's eyes glaze over and sometimes consign your application to the reject pile. And there's the other extreme: You get invited for an interview, but one of the interviewers is a psychiatrist. So applicants generally err on the overly cautious side, for fear of crossing the ambiguous boundary between creative/intriguing and worrisome/weird.

That's the primary value of this book: We hope it will show you how wide the boundaries are. We have assembled a variety of essays that helped their authors gain admission to some of the best medical schools in the country: Cornell, Harvard, Yale, Stanford, and many more. The essays are not all literary masterpieces, by any means. In fact, after you read seven or eight in a row, you'll gain sympathy for the admissions officers faced with a stack of 200 applications. But if you read them all, you should get an excellent sense of how you can craft your unique experiences into a coherent, interesting personal statement that reveals more about yourself than your grades and test scores ever could.

Be honest, be mature, be enthusiastic, and be sincere. Don't be afraid to go out on a small limb. Communicate your passion for medicine. Get noticed.

AN INTERVIEW *with a* DEAN

M edical schools have many methods for reviewing applications, though we found that most schools use a similar procedure to reduce the number of applicants to a reasonable pool from which to draw their incoming classes. This is not an easy task, since most schools receive thousands of applications for a first-year class of around 200 or fewer.

According to a recent *U.S. News & World Report*, the average acceptance rate for the twenty top medical schools is about 7 percent, with quite a few of the schools accepting only 3 percent of their applicants. With daunting figures like these, we asked med school deans and advisors about the importance of the essays in this competitive process.

Here's our composite version of an interview with a dean:

What is the difference between application essays for medical school and the essays we wrote to get into college?

The essays for medical school are more limited in scope. The college admission essay can often be about anything in the student's life, and applicants are encouraged to be creative, to have a "hook" that holds the reader. The essay for medical school, however, should be pointedly topical to medical issues. Essays that take the biggest risk are those that use creativity to do something different or unusual. This is usually not wise. Since it can be a turn-on or a turnoff, it's not worth the risk.

How are essays evaluated? By whom?

At selective medical schools, the process will be something like this:

There is a two-tiered system. First, the application materials are screened to determine who will be invited for an interview. Vanderbilt

School of Medicine, for example, receives about 3,500 applications for 104 slots. No medical school can offer an interview to every applicant. This primary screening committee, composed of the dean, the director of admissions, and one or two faculty members, utilizes the on-line application AMCAS (American Medical College Application Service), which contains one essay. For those students who have less than stellar numbers—i.e., less than a B average—the essay is moot. But for all candidates whose numbers are competitive for admission, every bit of the application is read.

The second tier—those invited for the interview—must complete the secondary application, which can require up to three more essays. A school may ask for a two-page autobiography, in which the student might say whatever he wants, and two shorter essays concerning any research experience the applicant has had and what it has meant to him, and any special skills that the applicant could bring to the medical school. A committee of three faculty members and perhaps one student will read these essays carefully, along with the rest of your credentials, and then, you hope, become your advocates. At this point, there can be some heated debate if there's a problem with the essay.

Do you want a description of a person, anecdotes of real-life experiences, or just a listing of accomplishments?

Descriptions and anecdotes, if they are relevant and well done, can have a positive effect on the overall quality of the essay. Since the accomplishments have been listed on the vitae sheet, rehashing them would not be useful, unless you make the right case. A good essay might very well repeat some accomplishments, but the difference will be in the treatment. You are writing a good essay if you are providing further description of exactly what you did, elaborating on what you got out of the experience, and defining what the experience meant to you.

Should this essay be about medicine?

It is important to link your essay subject to medicine. You may write a fascinating essay about your college baseball career, but it will be useless to your application if you don't make the connection to medicine.

There is room for some creativity here. For example, use college baseball to show the admissions reader how hand-eye dexterity, dedication, and teamwork are vital to becoming a useful member of a surgical team, a contributor in a research lab, or a person with the stamina for long hours on rotations. Tell us how your experiences will help you fit at our med school and become a great doctor.

Are there any hackneyed topics that applicants should avoid?

There is no stereotypical bad essay, but anything other than a straightforward narrative that responds to the question is risky. I'd say half of the essays I read concern a relative with a catastrophic disease. And these usually create the same problems: First, is the story true, or has the applicant exaggerated? And if it is true, these essays often reduce a major life turning point to maudlin clichés and trite generalizations. There's nothing inherently bad about the "disease essay," but applicants should consider carefully how they present the story.

Should applicants try to entertain you?

It depends. If you write well, if your narrative is full of details, if you can make your experience come alive for the reader in a way that's fresh and interesting, if it's relevant to your choice of a career in medicine—then it will be entertaining.

Here's what's not entertaining and therefore not smart: using or composing poetry inappropriately for an essay topic; talking about yourself in the third person, for example, "the future Dr. Quackensack"; describing your life through a book of fiction. And while we're on the subject of bizarre approaches, do not send CDs or videos.

Is motivation important? Do you want to see what an applicant plans to do with the degree?

No. An applicant should write about what's important to him, not what he thinks the med school wants to hear. The prospective student hasn't done rotations yet; he doesn't really know what's involved in each specialty, and until he does know, he shouldn't guess.

There are exceptions. For example, if your roommate has AIDS, and as a result, you have volunteered for AIDS-related service, worked in AIDS research, and perhaps published an article or written a senior thesis on the topic, then it has become part of your life and your credentials. Under such circumstances, it would make sense to write about your specific medical interest.

Do you want a good writer or a good person?

Yes to both. You are applying to a professional school; everything about your application should reflect that professionalism. A poorly or carelessly written essay will sabotage your chance for admission.

As for being a good person, most applicants say something about their desire to improve the quality of life. But if you present yourself as a person of compassion, be sure your records indicate the proof. If you talk the talk, show us that you've walked the walk. If your goal is to open a free clinic to provide health care to indigent patients, be sure in your vitae that all the volunteer work you've done with the homeless is clearly evident. Don't emphasize your compassion for humanity if the only volunteer work you've done is to dial a telephone for a fund-raiser.

One advantage to having a student on the admissions committee, as some selective schools do, is that the students can smell "folder filling" better than the faculty does. Your portfolio of activities should include the quality and quantity of volunteer service that reflect the person you seem to be in your essay.

What are you looking for in the application essay? Do you really consider applicants with liberal arts majors the same as applicants with science majors?

The answers to these two questions are related. They are connected by passion. The major is irrelevant, but it should be one about which you are passionate. Choose a major that excites you, then bring that excitement and that passion to the essay. Your passions should be coupled with what you have done with your life, and the essay is your best opportunity to convey that to the admissions committee.

The essay is also your opportunity for explanations. There are many nontraditional applicants to medical school: people who have chosen other careers before coming to medicine, students who have taken time off, or maybe traditional students with anomalies in their transcripts. Anything in your records that might raise a question with your readers should be addressed in the essay. You'll also have a chance in the interview, but the essay is still the best place to address a weakness.

For example, if you had a bad freshman year and the result is that your cumulative GPA is not where it should be, tell the committee the reason. An illness? Financial problems? A death in the family? If you don't explain, the weakness remains an obstacle to your admission. If you've taken time off after graduation, explain what you've been doing and how it brought you to medicine. If you've pursued another career, tell the committee about it.

If you have a perceived weakness in your application, make it your strength by addressing it head-on. If you don't, you have limited your chance of admission.

THE ESSAY QUESTIONS

The essay you will spend the most time sweating over—and probably the reason you bought this book—is the Big One: the AMCAS Personal Comments section. This section has no question, per se, to answer. Instead, you have one page to write basically anything you want about yourself. They do suggest you "consider" the following areas of inquiry:

- Why have you selected the field of medicine?
- What motivates you to learn more about medicine?
- What do you want medical schools to know about you that hasn't been disclosed in another section of the application?

The third question is really the key. On paper, many premedical students start to look identical. Most of them make good grades, volunteer in a hospital, and/or work in a research laboratory. To stand out from the application masses, you need to personalize your application with specific, unique details. What makes you exceptional and worth inviting for an interview? Why would the reviewer eventually want you to be his or her colleague?

The application also states that you may "wish to include information such as":

- Special hardships, challenges, or obstacles that may have influenced your educational pursuits
- Commentary on significant fluctuations in your academic record that are not explained elsewhere in your application.

This is also important. You don't want to leave lingering questions of the "What the heck happened here?" variety in the reader's mind. The admissions committee is looking for ways to reduce the pile of applications, so explain anything aberrant in your application clearly—and preferably without sounding like you're making excuses. Overcoming adversity can be a good thing when applying to medical school.

In its application for a recent entering class, AMCAS added a small secondary essay, entitled Practice Vision: "Describe your life and medical practice as you envision them ten years from now." This does not appear in later applications, but the topic could make for an interesting essay in your Personal Comments.

Secondary Applications

The process isn't over with the submission of your AMCAS application, because most schools have secondary applications. Some are sent to all applicants, some only to those who make the first cut. They range from a simple request for more money (averaging around $75) to "confirm your interest" in applying to their school, to multiple pages of extra information and essay questions. The questions typically seek additional clues for the admissions committee as to why you want to go to their school, whether you fulfill the needs of the school's mission statement, and why you want to pursue medicine in the first place. In addition, they are looking for notable items in your background that will distinguish you from other applicants and make the entering class more interesting and diverse.

Unlike the AMCAS personal statement, you don't have months to write and revise these essays. So we're giving you a head start: Here are some typical questions to ponder while you're waiting for the secondary applications to arrive. Of course, you could also use these questions as good starting points for your AMCAS essay.

• What are your reasons for applying to Acme Medical School?
• Please share with us something about yourself that could distinguish you from other applicants that is not addressed elsewhere in your application.

- Write an autobiographical statement, including family background and future career goals.
- What do you think you will like best/least about being a physician?
- Outline your skills, interests, aptitude, and personality in relation to your suitability for a career in medicine.
- What other career possibilities did you consider, and why did you reject them?
- If you had to choose a medical specialty today, what would you choose? Why?
- Highlight briefly your personal characteristics and experiences that are consistent with your area of medical interest.
- Describe your motivation to become a physician, including any disadvantages or obstacles.
- What do you see as the greatest challenge facing the medical profession today? What would be the best way to meet this challenge?
- Describe your exposure to the health care field. What insights have you gained about life as a physician?
- Describe the setting in which you envision conducting your medical career.
- Describe your major extracurricular activity. What special interests or talents have you sought to develop?
- How did you decide where to go to college?
- What is your assessment of your college experience?
- Describe any other areas in which you possess expertise or skill.
- What is your greatest academic/nonacademic strength/weakness? Why?
- If you have applied previously to any medical schools, what have you done since that time to enhance your application?
- What is the most meaningful volunteer experience you have had?
- Describe a way in which you've taken initiative or exhibited leadership.
- What personal characteristics make you effective in working with people?

- Who do you feel will be most likely to provide your personal support system while in medical school? Why?
- If you are not from [Big City/Middle-of-Nowhere], describe what personal experiences prepare you to live and study in [Big City/Middle-of-Nowhere]?
- Describe any personal circumstances indicative of some hardship.
- Tell us about a challenge you have overcome and what you learned about yourself from that experience.
- List the educational resources available in your home and community, and explain how you used them.

USING—*and* ABUSING—*the* INTERNET

The admissions officer is sitting at his desk, piles of papers everywhere indicating the degree to which he is overworked (or perhaps his own relaxed approach to organization). He is reading the forty-ninth essay of the day, when suddenly he has a wave of déjà-vu.

Now, he's been reading admissions essays at his private medical school for five years, and he's often read essays that remind him of something else. But this one—hmmmm:

New Albany City, check. Time, 15:30. Great! Reset timer; power normal; oil temperature, within range; compass setting, correct. Alone at 4,000 feet in a small airplane in a strange new territory and I am piloting my way perfectly. I feel like Lindbergh!

Is it possible that he's read about two student pilots this year? Coincidence? He thinks not. He reads through the essay about this young man's euphoric first solo flight and becomes more convinced that he has seen it before. He shuffles through the applications that he placed in a stack for a second review.

Bingo! There it is—the same essay in an application he read two weeks ago. Punctuation, paragraphing, wording, all exactly the same. He glances through the application. One academic recommendation mentions the flying lessons; the other one does not. Both applicants come from large urban areas, but not the same urban area, not even the same state. Both are bright students and quite tech savvy. Their undergraduate transcripts and their extracurriculars indicate a big interest in the Internet. In fact, one teacher recommendation names the computer as the culprit when her student misses deadlines or comes

12

to class unprepared. She intended to praise his expertise, but now the admissions officer is reading between the lines.

Taking a welcome break from his reading, he begins to surf the Net himself and quickly finds several Web sites that offer help for graduate school application essays. He investigates a few of the larger sites and finds one that will provide an essay of your choice on a variety of topics—for a fee, naturally. Thirty minutes later, he finds the exact essay the applicants submitted.

Both students are quickly rejected, of course. Furthermore, he "unofficially" alerts his admissions friends at the other schools indicated on the students' MCAT reports. It seems unlikely that either student will attend the medical school of his choice.

While this example is a compilation of several stories, the tale of the duplicate essay is absolutely true. Any dishonesty in connection with the application will prevent your admission to med school. If cheating is discovered after you've been accepted (and in one incident at Stanford, after a student had started classes), your acceptance will be rescinded.

While blatant plagiarism is rare, "canned" essays are becoming common. Increasingly, admissions officers are seeing the "packaging" of applicants. What has made this unhappy trend grow is the use, and abuse, of the Internet.

In one random search, we found almost 1,000 Web sites "guaranteeing" a winning application essay—college, law school, business school, dental school, you name it. One service offers a "final polish of the essay." This same site adds: "Unlike other sites, our editors do not merely write a critique of your essay; instead, they actually correct and make changes to your essay while maintaining your unique voice." This claim is, by definition, impossible; if your voice is unique, how can "they" duplicate it? "They" don't even know you!

Another service is even more blatant. Their Web site states: "We draft your university, graduate, or professional school essays or college admissions statements from the information you provide to us." Another one simply asks for your biography, and they take it from there. Be aware that while admissions readers are looking for your own voice, they're also pretty good at detecting when it's not there.

They want to see how you express yourself. As one admissions director said, "When that expression becomes a product of someone else's work, there's a word for that: *plagiarism.*"

The price for a graduate school application essay was around $500 and up, depending on how much assistance you receive and how fast you want it. The sites generally tout readers from schools such as Harvard, Yale, and Stanford, although there's no way to prove they have any affiliation with those schools—and chances are, they don't. Other sites are run by independent counselors (in one case, a mother who honestly admits she's just selling advice from her home) who charge fees for services that are provided free at most colleges and on many legitimate Web sites.

While many sites are perfectly honest, the Internet has provided almost unlimited possibilities for fraud. You can buy essays for as little as $15 from an "Ivy League" Web site, but beware. This same Web site buys essays. So if you purchase an essay, your medical school may have read that essay in the past, submitted by another applicant. Don't underestimate the intelligence of your admissions readers: They've been trained; they've read hundreds of essays before yours; and they know as much or more about the Web as you do. Remember, too, that many medical schools include current med students on the admissions committee. Your peers may be even more adept at smelling a canned essay than the professors are.

In fact, several Web sites, such as Plagiarized.com, help readers determine whether an essay is genuine, and there's software available specifically for detecting copied papers. Is it foolproof? Of course not. But is buying an essay off the Web a risk worth taking? Aside from the immorality of it, look at the practical aspect: If you submit a bad essay, it alone probably won't get you rejected. If you submit a plagiarized essay and it's discovered, you're immediately rejected—at that school, and probably at every school to which you applied.

Of course, cheating is not new, and it won't disappear. The Internet simply offers enticing new ways to lure even the best students into thinking they *need* an essay service, when, in reality, it's the last thing they need. None of the essays in this book are Pulitzer prizewinners, but they are honest products of the student. When an essay isn't, an admissions officer can smell it, and the results can be disastrous. And no one, no matter how desirable, is immune to close scrutiny on the essay. An admissions officer at Stanford recently said, "We just turned down an incredible prospect; the essays killed him." He went on to say that Stanford is seeing too much "editing" on student essays— sometimes the result of an overzealous school counselor, more often due to the growing influence of Internet sources.

An admissions officer from a private school in Georgia wrote

I had a case this year of a kid who stole an essay off the Internet and tried to pass it off as his own. It sounded familiar but I couldn't put my finger on it. I posted something on the NACAC [National Association for College Admission Counseling] Web site and within ten minutes people had sent me five or six sources. . . . by the way, I wrote a deny letter to him and a duplicate to his parents.

The Internet can provide terrific, legitimate suggestions and tips for all aspects of the application process, including the essay. The best place to start is at the med school's site itself. You can access any graduate school on-line by using the university's name, generally followed by ".edu." Read as much about the university as you can, including the questions they ask on their application. Familiarize yourself with whatever is unique about a specific institution. Ask yourself, "Why do I want to go to Takemeplease School of Medicine? How can I make a contribution there?" If you can answer that, you can probably write a good essay.

Many Web sites are excellent sources for all kinds of university and admissions data. For example, www.collegeboard.com (associated with the College Board, which is more than one hundred years old) has useful information about all aspects of the process, including preparing for the MCAT, applying on-line, writing the essay, getting financial aid, and even choosing the school that's right for you.

The National Association for College Admission Counseling (www.nacac.com) has great advice and links to other information sources, including essay help. Yahoo! offers several free services, some of which you register for, including MCAT tips and preparation, on-line applications, college searches, financial aid, etc.

The bottom line: Almost any information you want is available free on the Internet. But be careful, because the Internet alone can't get you through the application process. Not everything you see on the Web is valid or germane to your experience.

According to NACAC, more students are applying on-line every year. Critics say that some schools encourage on-line applications just to increase the number of applications they receive. This way, their well-publicized rejection rates will seem higher. Today, the majority of universities provide admission applications on-line. Almost every medical school applicant will submit a primary application on-line through AMCAS. At present, 114 medical schools use this service, which forwards your application, including the last three years of your MCAT scores, to the schools you designate. The current fee is $150 for the first application, and $30 each thereafter. The personal statement is on the AMCAS, so your first essay will be submitted on-line. Be extremely careful: There's no dress rehearsal; once you hit Send, it's gone!

Remember that all electronic resources begin with what you yourself contribute. There is still no substitute for self-discovery. What motivates you in your choice of med schools: Location? Reputation? Accessible professors? Class size? Career guidance? What is significant about the particular school you wish to attend? How does it seem right for you? The more you know about yourself, the more useful on-line information can be. As on-line applications increase, there will be more access to on-line aids—both honest and dishonest—for the application essays. The trick is to recognize the difference between helpful hints and outright cheating. Make your essay authentic. To be authentic, you shouldn't sound like a forty-year-old editor. Your own voice is your best chance of showing an admissions officer that you are special and that you belong at his school.

Most of the on-line services for graduate school essays charge a fee, but often these sites provide very helpful hints in their free material. The following is an excellent "Do's and Don'ts" list from Accepted.com:

The Do's

- Unite your essay and give it direction with a theme or thesis. The thesis is the main point you want to communicate.

- Before you begin writing, choose what you want to discuss and the order in which you want to discuss it.

- Use concrete examples from your life experience to support your thesis and distinguish yourself from other applicants.
- Write about what interests you, excites you. That's what the admissions staff wants to read.
- Start your essay with an attention-grabbing lead—an anecdote, quote, question, or engaging description of a scene.
- End your essay with a conclusion that refers back to the lead and re-states your thesis.
- Revise your essay at least three times.
- In addition to your editing, ask someone else to critique your personal statement.
- Proofread your personal statement by reading it out loud or reading it into a tape recorder and playing back the tape.
- Write clearly, succinctly.

The Don'ts
- Don't include information that doesn't support your thesis.
- Don't start your essay with "I was born in . . ." or "My parents came from . . ."
- Don't write an autobiography, itinerary, or résumé in prose.
- Don't try to be a clown (but gentle humor is okay).
- Don't be afraid to start over if the essay just isn't working or doesn't answer the essay question.
- Don't try to impress your reader with your vocabulary.
- Don't rely exclusively on your computer to check your spelling.
- Don't provide a collection of generic statements and platitudes.
- Don't give mealymouthed, weak excuses for your GPA or test scores.
- Don't make things up.

(This information is provided by Accepted.com, Inc. Further information is available at www.accepted.com or via E-mail at info@accepted.com.)

There are other helpful Web sites, as well. The following list can give you great advice and food for thought as you prepare to write your medical school personal statement. Check them out, but use surgically (pun intended):

- American Medical Association: www.ama-assn.org
- *The Journal of the American Medical Association:* www.jama.ama-assn.org
- Association of American Medical Colleges: www.aamc.org
- Columbia Undergraduate Student Affairs Pre-professional Office: www.studentaffairs.columbia.edu/preprofessional
- Premed.Edu Hunter: www.premed.edu/essay.html
- Medical School Application Essays: www.accepted.com/medical/index.htm
- Doc2be Pre-health News: www.fortisweb.com/doc2be
- All About Grad School.com: www.allaboutgradschool.com/usgrad schools/medical/medical.htm
- Premedical Handbook: www.puc.edu/faculty/Gilbert_Muth/hand book.htm; address is case sensitive
- Princeton Review medical section: www.princetonreview.com/medical
- Kaplan Test Prep and Admissions medical section: www.kaptest .com; click on "Pre-Med"
- *U.S. News & World Report* information and rankings: www.usnews .com/usnews/edu/grad/rankings/med/medindex.htm

While the Internet is an enticing tool, there's no substitute for simply reading real essays from real people. Take a hint from the examples collected here: Be yourself, whatever that may be. You're a college graduate; maybe you've already worked; maybe you already have a family. Your specific goal is to become a doctor. You have chosen to enter a noble, honorable profession. Take a risk. Let your essay show your potential for growth, for scientific inquiry, for contemplating new ideas, for change. Above all, be honest—to yourself, to your potential medical school, and to your own future.

THE ESSAYS

Leiomyomas, myometrial hyperplasia, osteoarthritis, serotonin autoreceptor transcription, xiphoid, omentum, vitiligo, drosophila—words that will drive your spell-check program crazy, but terms that many successful applicants to medical school are so familiar with, they use them in their personal statements and secondary essays. This points up the first similarity we found in the applicant essays: Almost all of them mention hospital or medical research experience.

There are other common traits worth mentioning. Most applicants have volunteered, usually in a medical field. Many have traveled to a poor region to perform some type of community service. Some have shadowed working doctors. A few have intriguing opening sentences:

- "For some time now, I have had to endure teeth-clenching pain on a weekly basis."
- "Who would've thought I'd spend two years of my life talking about parasites?"
- "The screaming of the little boy's mother shattered the relative serenity of the room."
- " 'American Invention to Destroy Sex,' the boy answered matter-of-factly."

Most essays reflect a person who is multifaceted, like the applicant who was a basketball player/motorbike mechanic/philosopher/would-be doctor. But within these common bonds, each successful applicant also must reveal his individuality, and the essay is the opportunity.

For organizational purposes only, we divided the essays into seven groups. These groups are artificial, so do not feel that you must write

19

an essay that would neatly fit into one of these categories. In fact, it was difficult to separate them, as most of the essays overlap in subject matter. They also share a tone of sincerity that is crucial. These are hopeful applicants who want to improve the quality of life. That's what has drawn them to this profession.

Since the authors of several essays requested anonymity, we occasionally deleted proper names and substituted a general name or date for a specific reference. However, our changes to the essays never distort the intent of the author.

Read Them All

Let's get one thing straight: The essays in this book are not standards that you have to meet in order to get into medical school. Some of you might have essays in your head far better than anything here. (If so, let us read them! See **www.essaysthatworked.com** for information on submitting your essays for the next edition of this book.) These are simply forty-one essays that worked, not the *only* essays that worked.

We hope that you will first read *all* the essays. There's a wide range here; some are 500 words, some are 5,000. Some have dialogue, some are aggressive, some are reflective. The question you should ask yourself as you read is not, "Is this a good essay?" but rather, "Do I get to know this writer from this essay?" If you are an admissions officer, you will also ask, "Now that I know this applicant, does he/she match my school?"

Getting into medical school is definitely not a writing contest; the competition is more subtle than that. More important than how well you write is how well you illustrate who you are and why a particular school is right for you. Believe it or not, the admissions officer wants what's best for you. With the ever-increasing quality of the applicant pool, most schools have little trouble filling their first-year classes. Your task is to communicate something new and meaningful about yourself to someone who knows you only by your numbers.

A Warning

Finally, a warning. We know that no one would be foolish enough to copy any of these essays verbatim. However, some of you might be tempted to take an essay and "change it around a little" to suit your application. We hope you know how stupid that would be. For one thing, stealing an idea or a phrase from an essay in this book would be dishonest. This type of "cheating" on the application will guarantee your rejection from the medical school. Stanford University rescinded admission to a first-year student two months into the academic year when they discovered the essay had been plagiarized.

Remember, this is a popular book. Many admissions officers have read it and are familiar with each essay. No admissions officer would ever admit a plagiarist.

The following is the story of an admissions counselor from a prestigious college who wrote to us after she learned we were revising the *Essays That Worked* series. The anecdote speaks for itself.

When I was associate dean of admissions at Georgetown in the (late 1980s), we were asked to select memorable essays from among the applications of students who were being admitted. Two enterprising Yale graduates had requested samples of "essays that worked" to publish in a guidebook aimed at a high school audience. Because of our involvement in the project, we received several complimentary copies of the volume, which I read out of curiosity.

This background knowledge proved useful during my tenure on the George Washington University admissions staff in a subsequent year. Imagine my surprise when I reviewed an application, only to recognize one of the examples from Essays That Worked. *Although the student had elaborated on the original theme, the initial paragraph was, word for word, part of an essay that appeared in the book.*

The student who plagiarized was unequivocally denied, even though he would normally have been a good candidate. Instead of increasing his chances of admission, he instantly destroyed the value of all his academic achievements over three and a half years. I shared with his college counselor the reason for our decision, knowing that the message would be relayed to the student. What a shame! He didn't trust his own ability to be impressive enough.

The following pages demonstrate the creative potential of the personal statement and the secondary essay. We hope these essays will inspire you when you begin to write, and we hope they will give you the confidence to write a bold, personal piece that is truly your own and help an admissions officer see why you are special. Enjoy the essays, study them, and let them be a catalyst for your own creativity.

I Want to Be a Doctor

So you want to be a doctor. That means you want to dedicate yourself to years of advanced training and exhausting days of studying, followed by intensive hours of on-the-job experience. You'll use more knowledge in one day than most of your friends needed for four years of college. The decisions you make will affect life and death, literally. It will be a long time before you have days off.

If what you know about being a doctor is defined by television and movies, you may want to think again. Difficult cases are not solved in sixty minutes (minus time for commercials). Most doctors are not, in fact, miracle workers. But if you've considered all this and if you are determined, you may become a very fine physician.

Virtually all the essays collected for this book were written by people who want to be doctors. Amidst the goals and descriptions of themselves, the authors chosen for this section seem to focus more on that message, but they don't all do it the same way. The admissions committee readers may be recent med school graduates, or even med students, and they'll be looking for evidence of your sincere enthusiasm for the profession. The more experienced faculty members on the committee will be moved if you can remind them of the excitement they felt as applicants or new doctors.

The first essayist, David E. Winchester, focuses on his volunteer activities, but he brings it nicely into synch with his desire to practice medicine. William Parker and Kristin Siegrist are very straightforward in their approach. They both claim in their opening lines that they have always wanted to be doctors. William was so certain that he applied for an Early Assurance Program, thereby committing himself to medical school much earlier than the usual applicant. Both of them support their claim with essays that trace the history of their deep-seated desire to be a doctor.

Glen Davis writes one of the best essays in this collection, both in content and composition. He uses Robert Frost (acknowledged in his opening words) and Henry David Thoreau (unacknowledged in his closing words) to trace the "itinerary" he took, both literally and figuratively, on his journey to medical school.

Using his passionate desire to return to his rural hometown and serve as a doctor there, the next writer creates an effective piece. Admissions committees are bound to take note of his ambition, as rural areas are notoriously underserved by committed physicians.

Finally, Eric Gordon never actually makes the statement, but he uses his essay to trace, with vivid attention to detail, the experiences that aroused in him the "passion" for medicine—which ultimately became a "calling."

The "I Want to Be a Doctor" approach is the most honest you can use, but it also has a lot of potential pitfalls. Be sure that you don't reduce your life's goal to a collection of clichés, stale sentiments, and arrogant statements about how you're going to save the world. Instead, focus on specific events that made you realize that practicing medicine is how you want to spend your life.

DAVID E. WINCHESTER

As I pulled on the brass door handle and slowly opened the massive wooden door, I motioned for Alex to go on inside. His face lit up with amazement. "Do those guitars and costumes really belong to KISS?" I told him yes, and he ran over to gaze at the glass case that enclosed a full drum set, costumes, guitars, and other memorabilia. Then the questions really started to pour from his head. "How did they get this stuff?" "What else do they have?" "Can I go look around?" As Alex wandered around the restaurant I sat at our table and reflected. I realized that while I have visited the Hard Rock Cafe many times, this was the first time Alex had been. It was thrilling to see him so overwhelmed at the experience. I thought to myself, this is why I volunteered to be a Big Brother, this is the kind of moment that I hoped would come from this experience. The joy of giving, especially because I gave him something that he could not have on his own.

That kind of satisfaction is one of the reasons that I want to be a doctor. It seems to me that being a doctor is one of the best ways to have that feeling in my life every day. It is that kind of feeling which reminds me of what it felt like doing rounds with my father in Tallahassee. I remember the way his patients would glow as we entered the room. He would introduce me and then they would chat for a while. The whole time we were with a patient, it was fascinating to see the way that they trusted him implicitly. They often fawned over us with their eyes as if to say "I'm so happy to have you here." It made them happy to have someone to put faith in. The entire experience was comforting.

I know that being excited about working with people and being able to bring them joy is not the only skill I will need to make a good doctor. Another personal quality of mine that I will use as a physician is my desire to continually learn. I am committed to using nearly every moment I have to learn. For example, one of the ways that I like to escape from schoolwork and other assignments is to read. Some of my favorite books include autobiographies of CDC [Centers for Disease Control and Prevention] epidemiologists and Stephen Hawking's *A Brief History of Time*. I read a lot of journals and newspapers, as well. I have also been teaching myself how to design Web sites and play the guitar.

As another way of learning, I try to make medicine part of my studies. The class I am enrolled in this summer has given me the opportunity to use sociology to study medicine. The major project in the class is to construct a survey to measure people's attitudes about a topic. My paper discusses how people's perception of their health changes with respect to their age, income, attitude about socialized medicine, and other variables.

Volunteerism is a quality that will be important as a doctor. I may have not had a lot of patient interaction and clinical experience, but that is not because I do not want to practice medicine. I was committed to other student groups before I learned about any decent opportunities to participate in clinical activities. I decided to stick with these activities because they not only benefited other students, but I learned a lot from them as well. I feel that my commitment to helping others and volunteerism is more important than where I chose to volunteer my time and energy.

My quality most beneficial to my future as a physician is my deep desire to practice medicine. In writing this statement, one of the exercises I performed to prepare was to brainstorm twenty-five reasons why I want to be a doctor. Some of the ones that stand out to me are "to make a difference," "to be a leader," and "to help people." In my estimation though, there is something even more important to notice than what the answers on my list were, and that is how easily they came. Once I started, the reasons just kept coming. In fact, I started the list with the goal of fifteen and I extended it because I was having so much fun daydreaming about being a doctor.

Daydreaming about being a doctor is not that new to me. Early in college, a friend and I were so captivated by medicine that sometimes, after class, we would go down to the Shands Teaching Hospital at UF [University of Florida] and give ourselves a tour of the OR. We would borrow scrubs from the locker room and go down the hall looking in the rooms trying to determine what the surgeons were busy doing.

When you add all of this up, what do you get? Take the satisfaction of bringing hope and joy to people, add a commitment to learning, throw in an unquenchable desire to practice medicine and you come up with me. I know that medical school is difficult but I welcome the challenge. After all, the benefits far outweigh the costs. It will be worth the hardships to hear from a patient the same sentiment that Alex leaves me with every week. "Thanks, Dave. I had a really great time today."

WILLIAM M. PARKER

Ever since I was twelve years old I've wanted to be a physician. I cannot pinpoint the specific event which sparked this unyielding desire; however, I do know what drives me in the direction of the health professions at this stage of my life. I've always enjoyed studying the sciences, especially those dealing with human anatomy and physiology. I also find a great amount of pleasure when meeting new faces and when helping others the best way I know how. Becoming a doctor, I believe, would thus be extremely satisfying and fulfilling, as I would be able to combine these three pleasures every day of my life. Also, every interaction I have had with the health professions (volunteering in the hospital, CPR training, viewing surgery from inside the operating room, etc.) has given me a feeling that has not and could not be matched by any other. Whenever I experience such interactions, I want to take what I've seen or learned to the next level. That is, I want to learn more about what is occurring and why. Going to medical school and becoming a doctor would enable me to do so, as well as to apply this knowledge to real-life situations.

I believe I have the stamina and willingness to make the commitment all physicians must make to their careers in order to succeed. An example of this stamina shows through during the cross-country season, when I need the energy to perform at practice and in the classroom. This summer was basically a duplicate of the school year, minus the schoolwork. I worked three jobs, including volunteer work, which equaled a minimum of fifty hours of work each week. In addition, summertime is cross-country's preseason; therefore, I ran five to ten miles each day. Many Tuesdays and Thursdays consisted of awakening at 5:30 A.M. to volunteer 7–11 A.M., working from 12 noon–6 P.M., conducting lead study interviews for the State Health Department

7–9 P.M., then running for an hour or more. These were the days I actually enjoyed the most. I enjoyed them not because I rose before the sun and continuously worked without a significant break, but because of the satisfaction and feeling of accomplishment they consistently generated.

Being accepted into the Early Assurance Program would allow me to participate in Le Moyne's Study Abroad Program in Australia. I have always wanted to visit a foreign country, and taking part in this program would fulfill this desire, along with allowing me to study in an environment aside from my own, presenting me with new and exciting challenges. More importantly, I believe studying abroad would permit me to experience new people and their culture, thereby expanding my knowledge of the world around me, and making me more understanding, in terms of people's different needs and beliefs. If not accepted into the Early Assurance Program, I would stay in Syracuse in the spring in order to better prepare myself for the MCAT. Further, I would need to be in Syracuse at this time, since I would be required to be interviewed by Le Moyne's Health Professions Advisory Committee, in order to apply to other medical schools.

KRISTIN SIEGRIST

My goal is to become a caring and competent physician who reaches out and makes a positive difference in the lives of her patients. As a child, I admired and trusted the physician who treated me when I was ill. He showed me the important role kindness and compassion play in making a patient feel comfortable and secure with the prescribed treatment. As I grew older, I developed an increased interest in the medical field as an exciting opportunity to help people directly to solve their problems, and in so doing, to change their lives. My decision to become a physician is based on numerous experiences, which have heightened my strong desire to make such an impact.

I have witnessed firsthand how one person can change the lives of others, simply through patience, understanding, and compassion. During high school, I participated in the "Peer Counseling" program, which was designed to develop and enhance effective communication skills, interpersonal skills, and community service participation by its members. I chose to touch the lives of children in the community by volunteering regularly in a local elementary school and at a nearby Boys & Girls Club, where I continue to serve. In addition, I also had the wonderful opportunity to work with elderly people for two years in a nearby retirement home. Caring for them in the dining room, and visiting them in their residences, I learned that simply by listening and using kind words and gestures, I formed many close relationships that have continued even today. Peer Counseling has definitely had a profound effect on my life and has shown me how rewarding it is to help others, and how easy it is to make a difference in someone's life. By becoming a physician, I can continue this work.

Due to limited family financial resources, even with several scholarships, I have had to continue working during college. For two years I have held a position as an elementary school reading tutor. Every time I work with these children, I know I am making a difference in their lives—not only with literacy, but also with motivation and self-esteem. The bonds we have created, along with the progress the children have made, are truly remarkable. With my extensive literacy training, I began working at the Shands Children's Medical Services Center, where I developed reading programs for children in the waiting room. While working there, I was also given the opportunity to take patients' vital signs, which gave me a great sense of purpose and satisfaction. During this period spent at the clinic, I became determined to enter the medical profession, and as a result, I pursued several opportunities to work or volunteer in medically related positions.

To become better acquainted with the medical profession, I volunteered at Shands Hospital in the Cuddler Program, where I held, fed, and changed newborn infants in the NICU when their parents were absent. I observed minor medical procedures and saw how the physicians explained to parents the status of their baby's health in such a way that assured them the baby would receive the best possible care. I also shadowed a family physician for over a year and observed his unique situations and procedures. Most importantly, I witnessed the sincere concern and honesty with which he treated his patients. By spending many hours talking with him and his patients, I developed a greater confidence that I possess qualities necessary to become an outstanding physician, such as good listening skills, effectual decision making, perceptiveness, and a genuine concern for others.

These traits proved to be invaluable when I later volunteered in the emergency ward at a local hospital. There, my greatest joy came from my interaction with patients, providing comfort and alleviating some of their pain. I had the incredible good fortune to work with a surgeon who treated me as a "student." He explained thoroughly during each patient's visit what symptoms were commonly seen, what preventive measures should be taken, and the treatment that should be given. His kindness, generosity, and passion for medicine made a strong impact on me.

These numerous work and volunteer experiences have helped me realize that medicine offers everything I want in a career—the ability to make a difference in the lives of others while working in a field which I find exciting, challenging, and rewarding. Becoming a physician provides the opportunity to have positive interaction with patients and create a doctor-patient relationship based on trust, communication, compassion, and confidence. My desire to positively influence the lives of others and my thirst for knowledge continue to direct me toward the medical profession.

GLEN DAVIS

W hen Robert Frost wrote about "the road less traveled," I am convinced he was thinking of the dirt path leading to Basma, a tiny village in the West African country of Burkina Faso, where the sight of a motorized vehicle is the talk of the town. I worked in Basma as a community health development volunteer with the United States Peace Corps—a road in my life that has, indeed, made all the difference.

However naive, I certainly *hoped* to make a difference when I went to Africa. But I also wanted to learn about medicine on a human level—beneath technology and bureaucracy—before forging ahead with formal medical education. My interest in medicine began during my senior year at Hamilton College. I started off as a student of the humanities, drawn to literature because I enjoy learning about people by reading about fictional characters. But as my professional goals evolved, I realized that I would rather contribute to the lives of *real* people in a measurable, humanitarian way. Since then, I have explored the medical profession as a postbaccalaureate science student at Bryn Mawr College, as a clinical researcher in a New York inner-city hospital, and as a health educator in rural West Africa. My road to becoming a doctor, though circuitous, has been uniquely my own.

Why, my friends and family demanded to know, did I insist on including the obscure country of Burkina Faso in my premed itinerary? Hot, flat, and famously poor, a capital city named Ouagadougou seemed an unworthy destination. But my years in the village of Basma profoundly impacted my personal and professional development. My home was a round, mud-brick hut on the grounds of the primary-care clinic, nestled between hospital rooms and the maternity ward, where I experienced the life of a "resident" in the literal sense of that word. Supervised by three African doctors, I assisted each day with clinical procedures and traveled to neighboring villages to vaccinate children against communicable diseases. My primary role was to work with village leaders to design and implement health education programs focusing on the following themes: prevention of malnutrition and dehydration; educating families about the vaccination schedule for communicable diseases; control and prevention of guinea worm disease; construction of latrines in family compounds to improve the health and hygiene of the village. My experience in Burkina Faso was an ideal precursor to medical school, introducing me to the nature of tropical diseases, clinical aspects of maternal and child health, public health theory in a real-world setting, and primary health care at the grassroots level.

But to speak of my three years in Basma only in terms of my work would give an incomplete impression of my life in Burkina Faso, for I lived my most memorable moments outside the clinic. I learned to conserve AA batteries by manually rewinding cassette tapes with a ballpoint pen. An apprentice to the village midwife, I mastered the art of holding the flashlight for a delivery while chasing chickens, goats, and pigs out of the room. Traumatizing children with the mere sight of my light skin, I experienced temporarily what it means to be a minority. Sipping millet beer with village friends under African skies, I was asked questions like, "Can you see the moon in your country?" I made bricks from the earth and built my own house with them, and I lived with bats, scorpions, and porcupines. Once a total stranger, with time I became a familiar friend, and I encountered goodness and integrity in people whom I will never forget. Warm and lively, with an enviable sense of humor and a dignified sense of who they are, the people of Burkina Faso sustain a moral wealth that makes economic poverty seem insignificant.

Since returning to the United States over a year ago, I realize how my work in Burkina Faso will enhance my study and practice of medicine. In my immunology course at the University of Pennsylvania, I remembered patients in Basma who died from malaria and meningitis, and I have insight into social factors that can influence the pathology of those diseases. In my work as a research assistant in emergency medicine at the Hospital of the University of Pennsylvania, the health care reform debate is all around me. I can evaluate various viewpoints based on personal recollections of the socialized medical system in the developing world. But ironically, it is the non-medical aspects of my service that will be most valuable to me in my career as a physician. Confined by cultural and linguistic barriers, I adapted to life in Basma and found common ground with people whose world is radically different from my own. I am likely to revisit that feeling when I adapt to life as a medical student and learn to provide comfort and support to patients. As I apply my experience in Africa to the classrooms and clinics that will fill my life for the next several years, I look forward to lifelong learning, to living fully and deliberately, and to dedicating myself to the health and well-being of others.

NAME WITHHELD

My desire to become a physician is one that has been gestating in me for as long as I can remember. However, it was only until the early part of my ninth-grade year that I realized rural family medicine was for me. I have virtually spent all my life in Geneva County, a small, rural Alabama county with a large majority of people living in what many would call poverty. It is out of growing up in this area, and seeing the lack of basic medical care for many citizens, that I desire to become a family practice physician and one day return to Geneva County and serve the people who have taught me so much.

In high school I had a wealth of opportunities to experience the role of a physician, and these experiences helped to change my initial unrealistic views concerning just what a physician does. After countless hours of interacting with doctors, nurses, patients, and other health care staff during my high school years, I developed a longing to work with others in a health care setting and to see that all people have access to health care. Over the course of my undergraduate education, I had many opportunities to work in a variety of health care settings. From the practices of rural family physicians, to a hospice organization, to a large trauma unit, I have gained a plethora of knowledge and insight concerning the field of medicine.

However, in all of these settings, one sudden realization still rings true, and that is there is no greater satisfaction in this world than helping people through the practice of medicine. I have seen frowns turned to smiles of comfort when a physician walks into a patient's room. I have experienced emergency room physicians gently embracing an accident victim's family and have seen the relief a family receives from this simple action. My involvement during my undergraduate career with various health-related organizations made me more inclined to the personal qualities a physician should possess. I have been awakened to the enormous responsibilities a physician faces daily and have seen the vast importance of healthy doctor-patient relationships. Over the past eight years, I have taken every advantage offered to me and have tried to fully understand just what it takes to be an effective physician.

Through these experiences, I have come to the conclusion that not just one or two traits make up an effective physician. A physician must possess a certain degree of intelligence and curiosity. On the other hand, I have learned that sensitivity, compassion, and diplomacy also play a major function in making a good doctor. In addition, an effective physician must be totally committed to the practice of medicine and to the overall well-being of his or her patients. Through various health-related activities over the past eight years, I have experienced what it takes to be an effective physician. While the "ideal" physician cannot be created overnight, I will be able to draw upon my experiences to help bring out these qualities and characteristics within me.

Currently, as I pursue a Master's of Public Health degree in Health Policy and Management at Emory University, I am being awakened more than ever to the big picture of health care and the lack of basic health services in rural communities across America. Also, by working at the national office of the American Cancer Society as a public health intern, I am beginning to understand the implications of disease and how they affect society. By obtaining my MPH degree, I will be a stronger voice for rural medicine and will possess the "tools" to do more for the cause of rural medicine, along with serving the basic health needs of a rural community. Many of the qualities that rural living offers are simply unsurpassed. However, there is a need for better, more encompassing health care in rural communities. Clearly, the lessons and experiences I am receiving this year at Emory and the American Cancer Society will be a tremendous asset in the future as I one day serve as a rural health care provider.

Culminations of experiences, lessons, and other events have drawn me ultimately to pursue a career in medicine as a rural family practice physician. However, I do not particularly view being a physician as a career choice, but rather as a calling. I sincerely possess the desire to serve others and be a vehicle in restoring health as a physician. My compassion, commitment, and energy to the field of medicine will allow me to become an effective physician. Many will tell you that I am too passionate about becoming a doctor. Yet, I understand what a tremendous difference a physician can make upon society and I am humbly ready to contribute in this capacity. In closing let me say that you will never encounter someone who truly wants to serve a rural community as a physician more than I. I am totally committed and dedicated to going the distance to become a rural health care provider and look forward to the day when I can start medical studies.

ERIC GORDON

For two nights I got very little sleep, tossing and turning with the vivid images of what I had seen. It happened on a Friday afternoon, my first day of training for a volunteer position in the department of surgery. After four months in the emergency room, recommendations from my supervisor, and an interview, I was wearing scrubs and learning the art of transporting patients to and from surgery. Our last patient of the day was already in a stretcher when we met him at the elevator coming up from the ER. He was covered with lines and wires, and was being carefully monitored by three nurses. As we quickly moved down the long corridor back toward the surgical suite, my job was opening doors. It was exciting for me to know that although medically speaking I was useless to this poor man, my presence was nevertheless helpful and appreciated. By the time we had turned the last corner his moaning had grown to yelling and then gurgling because he vomited.

Up until that point I had only seen an operating room from the outside. After putting on a mask, I opened my last door, completing my job for the day. Then I received some final instructions: "You can stay and watch if you stand in that corner and don't touch anything." For five hours I stood in that corner of the room, which was cold except for the heat radiating from the lights and instruments that had just come out of the autoclave.

The incision ran from the xiphoid to below the umbilicus, and within minutes the surgeon had reached his destination, a massively ruptured aortic aneurysm. Below the bright white surgical lights were those vivid images that kept me awake: glistening yellow omentum, gray intestines, which were slowly and rhythmically contracting—all surrounded by pools of bright red blood. What an awesome sight to see the inside of a living human being surrounded by others working desperately to preserve that life. I still stand amazed.

A hospital is a very special place to work. For many it is the first and last stop they will make during their lifetime. To be a part of those moments as well as the many moments of need in between is truly a privilege. I look forward to the role of physician in the lives of people who are willing to be helped, as well as those who may not want help, whether it be a child with a cough or an old man like the one described above. By doing my job I will know that I am making a difference in people's lives.

Over the past two years my desires to practice medicine have consistently grown and solidified. Volunteering and later working at Memorial Hospital was a wonderful learning experience when it came to both medicine and people. In August, the setting for my education switched to the classrooms of Barry University, where I have enjoyed and excelled in courses very similar to those taught in the first year of medical school. Through these experiences, I can say with total sincerity that I have a passion for learning about the human body and the science of medicine. I am excited to continue on this journey in medical school, training for that to which I believe I am called.

I Don't Want to Be a Doctor

Not everybody knows from birth what he wants to do with his life. John Locke maintained environment and experience fill in the tabula rasa with which we are born, while John Calvin believed our lives are predetermined. Somewhere between the dueling Johns are medical school applicants who found their calling after pursuing other interests. Had any of them been asked about med school a few years before applying, they would have said, "No, I don't want to be a doctor." These are students who did not feel that medicine was their destiny, at least not at first.

Honesty is always the best policy—especially in admissions essays, where it's also refreshing. Don't be afraid to write about your experiences and interests, even if they don't reflect a genetic predisposition toward a career in medicine. Remember, one of your goals is to let the readers know what makes you tick, what excites you, what choices you've made. How and why have you arrived at the momentous decision to apply to med school? Obviously, your passion at some point turned to medicine, but maybe by a circuitous route. The essay is your chance to tell the committee exactly how that happened—and to make them root for you as you tell your story.

The essays collected here all describe applicants who either resisted a medical path or began pursuing careers outside medicine. Note, however, that the essayists use those earlier pursuits to connect to—and enhance—their eventual decision to become doctors. In the first piece, Lakshmi Swamy's mother was a doctor, and the difference between her grueling schedule and Lakshmi's impression of medicine from the glorified images she saw on TV made her seriously doubt whether medicine was right for her. Her determination to be a doctor grew with time and travel. Next, Scott Rickert was training for a career in physics, well on his way to being published in his field, when he made important self-discoveries that led him to medicine.

Louise King was also inspired by her mother, an attorney. Louise became a practicing lawyer and then went back to school to get her prerequisites to apply to med school. Notice how she traces the similarities of interests that drew her from one field to another. Using a childhood toy as an effective metaphor, Afshan Ahmad makes a clear case for the value of pursuing history and science to become a doctor who can communicate with patients with sensitivity and perspective.

Jessica Weisz and Louis B. Lin write brief, pointed essays about their change of heart. Jessica was determined to pursue a public policy career and joined the Peace Corps. Through that experience, she learned she wanted more involvement in primary care. So back she went to undergraduate school. Louis, a self-proclaimed product of the business 1980s, admits up front that "attending medical school was just an afterthought." He, too, followed another career path first, but he describes how he can use his business experience to become a more effective physician.

The final essay is poignant. The writer suffered a frightening disease, her father was a doctor, and her interest was science. But until she realized the importance of patient care, she was not moved to pursue medicine. The humanitarian motivation of a prospective medical student is vitally important. This writer's case was strong enough to gain admission to nine highly ranked medical schools.

Don't be discouraged if you didn't grow up wanting to be a doctor. Instead, use your essay to draw connections between your first career choices and medicine. It would be a big mistake to ignore a decision of this magnitude in the essay, thereby leaving an unanswered question in the mind of the admissions reader.

LAKSHMI SWAMY

"Resuscitation"

Annie was not breathing, nor did she have a pulse. True, she was only a dummy I met while taking my CPR certification course, but I could not help thinking, "What if she were a real person?" The question stayed with me for the rest of the day, and I was not sure if I could have saved her life.

This was not the first time I had doubted myself. Inspired by television documentaries showing open-heart surgeries and life as an emergency room doctor, I started considering a career in medicine while in high school. However, these edited portrayals of physicians contradicted impressions of my mother, a doctor, leaving our house at 3 A.M. to attend to patients at the state-run psychiatric hospital across the street. I was disheartened by the despair and isolation that she faced in her patients every day. By the time I entered the University of Georgia, I had mixed emotions about my career choice. I needed to form a realistic impression of the medical profession. Fortunately, through my research stipends from the Foundation Fellows Scholarship, I have had the opportunity to remedy these doubts—while traveling in Europe, South America, and the Caribbean.

My serious interest in medicine took shape ninety miles off the coast of Florida. I was intrigued by Cuba's health care system, which, despite a severe lack of resources, maintains the general health of its people at a level characteristic of developed nations. My curiosity led to daily visits to family doctors, polyclinics, and hospitals during my one-week stay in Cuba. These informal meetings with physicians and patients revealed to me the important role that preventive medicine plays in the Cuban health care system. The success of preventive care, I realized, is based largely on the Cuban people's great trust in their health care professionals. This trust was quite apparent in Maria, a woman I met at the Alternative Medicine Clinic outside Havana. I put my knowledge of Spanish to use when I asked her why she was there. Maria explained that she was being treated for vitiligo. "The doctor is working miracles," she said, as she showed me her face and hands where the disfiguring white patches were slowly regaining pigment. Talking to patients like Maria helped me to realize that, although I am sometimes saddened, I am not uneasy listening to stories of illness and complaints of pain. Later that day, I toured the clinic with its director, eighty-year-old Dr. Juventino Acosta, who stressed the importance of emotional support and counseling in Maria's treatment. Whenever I hear the phrase *bedside manner*, I think of Dr. Acosta, the jolly doctor greeting each patient by name and constantly reminding me how to "treat the whole person." His passion for medicine was infectious.

I returned from Cuba hungry for more contact with the medical profession. When presented with such an opportunity in Heidelberg, Germany, I did not hesitate to accept it. While there, I lived in the nurses' dormitory of Bethanien Geriatric Hospital and worked on a suicide epidemiology project at the University of Heidelberg. After long days at work, I spent my evenings keeping patients company on the third-floor ward. I enjoyed the simple services that I could provide just by helping them walk down the hall or by listening to their stories of World War II. Over the course of three months, I became familiar with the hospital environment, I befriended a few of the patients, and, in the process, I improved my German language skills.

As I was exposed to different aspects of medicine during my travels, it became increasingly easier to think of myself as a doctor someday. Still, I needed to test my resolve by returning to the issues that had made me initially question a career in medicine. I recently accompanied my mother on several occasions when she was on call at the admissions office of Central State Hospital, the psychiatric institution in my hometown. As she met with incoming clients throughout the night, I had the chance to revisit, in a clinical setting, the mental health issues that I had first encountered through my epidemiological study of suicide in Germany. The stresses of my mother's job were apparent to me as I saw her deal with the indigent, the abused, and the violent. I realize that any field of medicine has its tragedies. Now that

I am aware of some of the challenges inherent to the practice of medicine, I can say that I am willing to accept them.

Looking to my future, I am constantly reminded of how much I have to learn before I can perform a psychiatric evaluation as my mother does or treat a patient with vitiligo as Dr. Acosta does in Cuba. I consider my studies in microbiology and computer science, my internships, my research, and my travels as a toolbox of experiences that I will take with me to medical school. One could say that my commitment to a career in medicine has been resuscitated—I could indeed save Annie's life.

SCOTT RICKERT

High up in the Venezuelan Andes, staring through the eyepiece of a five-ton Schmidt telescope, I made the decision to leave physics. I had been working on Yale's groundbreaking astrophysics project for two years (publishing credits pending) and though I thoroughly enjoyed the scientific research, there was something fundamental missing. Only in the thinned Venezuelan air did I put my finger on it. In the small town of Mucuchies, the site of the telescope, I became much more interested in the local people than the science I came to perform. I noticed many small details about the local people, such as how the thin air at that altitude gave them rosy cheeks. Fascinated by their culture, I spent hours talking in broken Spanish, French, and English trying to understand whatever I could. It was the Andean health and nutrition, the bare living conditions, and the smatterings of Spanish that lingered with me after I returned. I realized that the fundamental missing piece in my scientific career was the need to interact with people of all walks of life. Although I had not yet definitely decided to become a doctor, my path toward medical school became inevitable.

This interest in people had been developing for a long time. I enjoyed studying physics in my four years at Yale. I received distinction in the major, spent a summer working on the design and construction of Yale's solar-powered vehicle, and worked as a researcher in astrophysics. I felt I learned most, however, from my humanities classes: a summer in London studying literature, courses in Greek and Dutch art. They expanded my ability to think critically, and revealed to me again and again that I was as much interested in people as in quarks.

Returning from Venezuela, I changed my life drastically. I resigned my position as an Assistant Research Scientist at Yale's physics department, gave up my deferred Ph.D. fellowship, and before long was taking courses in biology and chemistry. Basic scientific research, while essential for our society, was no longer what I wanted to pursue. I wanted to use my scientific skills to help others through direct personal contact.

To support myself, I worked at the Harvard Graduate School of Education as the Personal Computer and Network Specialist. What I originally thought would just be a paycheck turned into a great training ground for dealing with people in crisis. I was responsible for over 400 people's computers. When fixing any computer problem, large or small, I always made an effort to sit down and explain to the person what went wrong with the computer, why, and how I would fix it. I felt that while my job was to fix computers, it was also important to reassure the person involved. I enjoyed using my scientific problem-solving skills to help those in difficult situations.

I also began volunteering at Brigham and Women's Hospital in the Intensive Care Units of Surgery and Burn and Trauma. As a family liaison, I consoled and assisted the families put in the difficult situation of having a family member in the ICU. While the doctors and nurses dealt with the patients' physical needs, I gave the families emotional support. This involved anything from directing them to the cafeteria to talking with them about whatever was on their minds—from their tough drive home to the difficult decision of whether to remove life support from a terminal family member. This work was extremely satisfying personally. I was moved and challenged by this experience: the weekly interactions with the longer-term families; the Smiths' bursting cheers when their sister was transferred to a normal hospital room on the road to recovery; the grief of the Joneses when their father passed away; the overall challenge to me of working in a stressful situation. This solidified my decision to pursue medicine as a career. The combination of challenging scientific problems, intense personal interactions, and personal satisfaction was exactly what I wanted.

This upcoming year, I plan to continue pursuing my long-term medical goals. I have tentative arrangements to work in a general surgery unit in both patient care and research. Late next spring, I also plan to combine my technical skills with my health interests to set up a computer-linked worldwide tracking program for the World Health Organization. At the very least, I will continue volunteering.

I believe that my combination of strong research and technical skills, a deep interest in personal interaction, and a focused desire to be working in medicine will serve me well as a doctor. My wide range of experiences will allow me to serve my patients with intelligence, patience, and passion—whether they are from the Andes or anywhere else in the world.

LOUISE KING

I stood over a boy, no more than fifteen. He was drunk and appeared to be in immense pain. He lay sprawled across a cot in the
corner of a room that had begun to smell strongly of stale alcohol and
urine since his arrival. His clothes were filthy and I thought he must
have lived on the street. Suddenly, my eye was drawn to his right arm
that seemed discolored and somehow deformed. Dr. Jan Singh stood
next to me and explained that he was a glue sniffer, a common problem in Quetzaltenango, Guatemala. He had suffered severe burns
when he had attempted to heat glue so as to better inhale the fumes.

Jan and I, along with other doctors and volunteers, had come to
Guatemala to distribute medicine, medical care, and other aid. I had
originally been assigned to help the construction crews, but Jan had
recruited me as an all-purpose translator and medical aide. I had only
just learned some rudimentary Spanish and had a vague recollection
of first aid training from close to ten years before. Despite my inexpe-
rience, I felt comfortable helping Jan. While working in Guatemala, I
saw a small child with worms growing under his scalp, and I helped to
extract them. I helped a man, again smelling strongly of alcohol, into
the treatment room and naively struggled with him to remove his
jacket from over his arm only to discover he had broken it a few days
before and was embarrassed by the state of it. I took pictures for the
doctors' records of one woman with herpes sores that covered nearly
all the skin of her cheeks and of another whose arthritis had crippled
her hands.

These sobering experiences aside, the sight of the young boy on the
cot remains my most vivid memory from Guatemala. The extent of
his injuries shocked me, especially in contrast with his youth. I believe
my memory of him is so vivid because we were unable to help him.

Although we did find him a bed in a local hospital, he left the next night, before the doctors were able to begin treating his arm. We looked for him around the city but never found him. When I first saw him in the room, however, I was excited by the thought of helping him. I had no idea how I could help, given the severity of his burns, but the mere possibility inspired me and still does. At the same time, my excitement felt bittersweet as I was scheduled to begin classes at law school a month later. I couldn't imagine being able to help people as an attorney in the same tangible way as I was able to help them in Guatemala. I spoke at length with Jan and others about my feelings. Jan expressed her opinion that a lawyer could just as easily help as a doctor could. She advised me, as did others, to attend law school. I had seen my mother help countless defendants as a public defender in California, so I set out for law school convinced that Jan was right.

In a way, she was. As an attorney, I have been able to help. By writing bench briefs for the Louisiana Supreme Court, I played an important role in ensuring that justice was done in individual cases. In my pro bono work in Texas, I have had the honor of helping individual families through hard times. Being thanked by them personally is the best reward. But I have never forgotten Guatemala and how I felt when I worked there. Although I have lost touch with Jan, I remain inspired by my memories of her work with patients and the insights I achieved while working with her. I have incorporated these skills into my practice of law and have relied on them when interviewing legal clients. Looking back, however, the most important lesson I learned is how much I enjoy working with people in the unique way that a health professional can.

In the past year and a half, as I have completed my prerequisites, I have rediscovered a love of science I had lost in college. My grades at the University of Texas at Dallas reflect this rediscovery. Moreover, during my volunteer work in the Parkland Hospital ER and my time as a research assistant for Dr. Thomas Andrews, I have explored different areas of medical practice. Invariably, I have found myself yearning to learn more and to participate at a higher level. What fascinates and drives me is the possibility of choosing a career which combines both science and the art of helping those in need.

In short, I have followed a circuitous and complicated path to achieve a dream I've had since my time in Guatemala and before, but it was the perfect path for me to take. I am especially grateful that the path I chose passed through law school as the skills I learned there are invaluable for my future practice of medicine. Moreover, I needed my time in law school and thereafter to gain confidence in my abilities, to develop my sense of personal integrity, and to truly commit myself to what will be a long road through medical school and on into a career as a doctor.

AFSHAN AHMAD

My first toy was a Fisher-Price stethoscope. I think my parents, who are both pediatricians, bought it for me before I was born. I carried my favorite toy with me everywhere. Whenever I found a free moment, I examined the bright orange earpieces and noticed how a separate blue hollow cord originated from each neon sphere. Tracing the blue cylinders with my fingers—one tube with my left hand and the other with my right—my hands would inevitably meet as they neared the chest piece. I wondered how two separate paths could converge to a single one that would allow me to listen to someone's heart.

When it was time to put my beloved stethoscope aside, my curiosity turned to my surroundings—namely, my peers. I became enthralled with the chemistry and biology of the human form. The summer after my sophomore year at college, I took biology before I left for a year abroad. Although I enjoyed science throughout the school years, covering a year's worth of biology lectures and labs in nine weeks in a competitive environment, I suspected, would make for a significantly less pleasant experience. One day I walked into class after spending two nights awake studying for the final and completing two daunting labs. I arrived at this Tuesday lecture late and dreary-eyed to find my peers silent and writing: The professor had surprised the class with a pop quiz. Mustering up what little energy I had left, I trudged to the nearest teaching assistant and began the quiz. To my surprise, the questions did not ask for a repetition of facts as they normally did, but instead forced me to apply my knowledge in an innovative fashion to solve problems that did not resemble lecture or textbook questions. By the final question on DNA transcription, I found myself grinning. I had forgotten about the fatigue and simply enjoyed the challenge of the questions I read. Moreover, I thrived on the complete immersion into a subject that stimulated my intellect.

However, science alone did not satiate my curiosity about human nature. I grew intrigued by the complexity of human behavior so I devoted myself to the humanities, especially history. Examining human behavior in countless times and cultures, I gleaned insight into multiple perspectives. Pursuing history at Oxford University enriched my academic knowledge and challenged my intellect in unprecedented ways. Interacting with my English peers and tutors, I also understood how differently we viewed the same world. I was so awestruck by this notion that when I returned to Northwestern University, I wrote an honors thesis on the changing travelers' views of Renaissance Venice. After living abroad and writing my history thesis, I have a greater appreciation for the multiplicity and influence of individual perspectives.

Peers, professors, and family members were surprised by my pursuit of two seemingly divergent paths but it is my interest in both science and history that has led me to medicine. As the separate blue cords of my childhood toy converged to a single tube that allowed me to hear someone else's heartbeat, the combination of my different intellectual interests drives my fascination with medicine. The medical field is not strictly about science but rather it centers on the patient and therefore humanity. I believe my study of history and living abroad will help my future patients. Through broadening my academic scope, I honed a diverse range of skills, including verbal abilities as well as scientific adeptness. Everyone is well aware that a doctor's scientific ability and analytical skill must be exceptional. However, I have observed people who forget that physicians must have strength of character and outstanding communication skills as well. Physicians interact with people who are often in their most vulnerable states. In order to communicate in the most gentle, honest way possible, the physician must be able to articulate a diagnosis, prognosis, and plan for treatment in precise terms that can be understood by patients of diverse backgrounds and perspectives. The basis of sensitive communication is the ability to see outside one's personal views and empathize with multiple perspectives—an ability I have cultivated throughout my undergraduate career.

I understand that being a physician demands an unfaltering commitment to heal and a keen aptitude for the sciences. What distinguishes the excellent physician from the average one is not only quickness and accuracy of diagnosis, but also the ability to connect with patients on an intimate, comfortable level through caring communication. It is my studies in history and my Oxford experience that give me the potential to succeed in this aspect of medicine. I recognize that becoming an ideal physician is not an easy task but I look forward to the challenges that lie ahead as I pursue a career in medicine.

JESSICA WEISZ

Who would've thought I'd spend two years of my life talking about parasites?

Well, as an undergraduate at Penn State, it wasn't my first thought either. At the time, I was studying health policy, a field I enjoyed but found lacking in hands-on practical involvement. I wanted to remain in the health field, but desired a discipline in which I would interact directly with patients. I explored many opportunities: I did some work in rehabilitative physical therapy; I taught for the American Red Cross; I became a youth worker in a residential treatment facility for abused adolescents. Each experience gave me more insight into what would eventually be my final career decision, but none so much as my experience as a Health Volunteer in the United States Peace Corps.

Thanks to the Peace Corps and an incredibly supportive network of family and friends, I spent two years in Ecuador teaching mothers, midwives, and health promoters how to improve nutrition, hygiene, and sanitation in their homes and communities. I worked with a local doctor, psychologist, and nurse team conducting vaccination campaigns and building latrines in communities where none had previously existed. I led health talks for groups of women and teenagers about reproductive health and sexually transmitted diseases in order to increase their awareness and usage of contraceptive methods. A mutual trust developed; the women often invited me into their homes to talk about their fears of menstruation, pregnancy, and the health of their children. Given an opportunity to fulfill their needs as a health educator and compassionate friend, I began to see health care on a more individual level. As I became more involved with my community, I spent less time thinking about the comforts of unlimited electricity and indoor plumbing and more time weighing babies, treating dehydration, and talking about parasites. I saw many things for the first time: the birth of a baby, the effects of severe malnutrition, and the death of an eight-year-old girl due to respiratory failure. I became fascinated by the body's ability to function, reproduce, and heal. Biological phenomena inspired me, and I wanted to learn more.

As my Peace Corps service neared its completion, I made plans to enroll in the Harvard University postbaccalaureate premedical program. While it was intimidating to return to undergraduate courses, I knew my life experiences would serve as a solid foundation, not a setback. At the end of summer session, my mentor invited me to spend a week shadowing a first-year resident. The exposure to illness and treatment in an urban teaching hospital was a stark contrast to my rural health experience. The patient population, the physician protocol, and the availability of medications differed enormously. Yet, in both environments, the physician served as a healer, a teacher, a leader, and a friend. I returned to Harvard with a renewed interest in and dedication to medicine.

From Ecuador's flying ants and barb-bearing scorpions to Harvard's physics and biochemistry, I have gained insight into my capacity for responsibility, commitment, and perseverance. My experiences have prepared me for the challenges of a career in medicine.

LOUIS B. LIN

I have to admit that for most of my life, attending medical school was just an afterthought. Being a child whose formative years were spent in the roaring 1980s, I firmly believed a career in business was the way to go. It also did not hurt that my father, a research biologist, insisted that I head toward a career in corporate America, flush with income tax loopholes, generous expense accounts, and substantial year-end bonuses.

Shadowing an otolaryngologist in high school only reinforced my suspicions that medicine was not the way to go—after a few short days I contracted a severe cold from one of my mentor's patients. By this time, the excesses of the 1980s gave way to the Internet boom of the 1990s. With managed care deeply entrenched, it was clear to me that medicine was taking a backseat.

I cannot say that there was any single event that led to my decision to pursue a career in medicine, but that my life experiences, consciously or not, have been inexorably linked to the field. Even as a business minor in college, I never lost sight of my interest in medicine. Whether it was the summers I spent working for biopharmaceutical firms attempting to unlock the secrets of human illness or creating a new course at Berkeley covering the role of biotechnology in science and health care, many of my activities have been based on the premise that medicine and the biological sciences will improve humanity.

Despite my initial role in marketing and business development at a start-up medical device firm, I found myself drawn to the medical research aspect of the company—developing a new device platform to remove cardiovascular calcification. From my work experience I have learned to appreciate the interdisciplinary opportunities physicians have to directly and indirectly impact many lives through patient care and entrepreneurial therapeutic development. I can now also appreciate how my interest in business has not gone to waste, for medicine's new emphasis on cost-effective yet compassionate care will require a new business sense if physicians are to successfully navigate the managed care environment and create the next generation of efficient medical technologies. With this in mind, it is clear to me now that medicine appeals to me because it is a combination of science and business that offers a wide range of meaningful career opportunities.

Although I reside in Silicon Valley, where young people like myself seem increasingly flush with Internet riches, I choose medicine. My experiences as a volunteer at the Veterans Hospital with exposure to chronic care has made me realize that although I am surrounded by materialism, the look of relief on a patient's face cannot be purchased. I choose medicine because I know I can make a real difference—not just one that lasts until the next product cycle.

NAME WITHHELD

T he path to the basic research laboratory where I have worked for the past three years crosses the entryway to Children's Hospital. There are few sights more heart-wrenching than a sick child, and many ailing children cross this busy intersection each day. I often smile at these young patients and many of them smile back, despite being confined to wheelchairs or walking with an IV pole close behind. I greet these sick children with a special understanding, having myself been diagnosed with Graves' disease at the age of eight. The problem was subtle, and it was not until I visited a seasoned pediatrician who noticed my enlarged thyroid that the diagnosis was made. I still remember my fears as a child undergoing a battery of tests, lying on cold examining tables with huge machines whirring all around me. Fortunately, I received excellent medical care and my illness was easily controlled with medication. Such an experience might have set me on the path of becoming a physician, to give the best possible care to those who might not have as supportive a family or access to outstanding medical care. The fact that my father is a physician might have pushed me even more in this direction, yet I did not decide on medicine until I started college.

My original career goals were quite different; I wanted to be a laboratory scientist. The summer after my sophomore year in high school, I traveled to Michigan State University for an NSF [National Science Foundation] internship in an organic chemistry lab. Though initially daunted by the mess of lines and letters that represent organic compounds, I struggled to learn the language of organic chemistry and was able to help my lab group make significant progress on the synthesis of an antileukemia molecule. My exit evaluation praised my motivation, and my professor noted that two months before, I wouldn't have been able to understand—much less give—my own final presentation of my work. While working in the laboratory that summer, I began to contemplate the possible applications of the antileukemia compound we were attempting to synthesize. This kind of cancer research might one day be used to treat people like my grandfather, who was dying from lymphoma that same summer. Though he himself remained in good spirits, joking with his doctors about being a "lymphomaniac," I felt frustrated that cancer research was thus far unable to save him.

When I started college, I was still committed to continuing in basic research, but with the added goal of using my work to help patients like my grandfather. I arranged a meeting at a laboratory whose HIV and cancer research fascinated me. As I left Dr. Smith's office after my interview, I knew this was the lab for me. His research in hematology and oncology was cutting edge, but that was not what sealed my attachment to Dr. Smith and his work. Unlike other laboratories, which focused solely on data, his weekly lab meetings routinely featured discussions of patients. Dr. Smith was the first lab chief whom I had ever heard discuss research work in the context of his patients, and this was the first time I truly grasped the tight link between research and patient care. It felt humbling to look at the stacks of T-cell cultures and to realize that their contents might one day be applied to treat patients with cancer or HIV. Since no amount of research data can ease the mind of someone who is sick, it must be the doctor who bridges this gap by tending to the patient "both in body and in soul," as Dr. Smith is fond of saying. Working in the laboratory has been invaluable to me, teaching me the rigor of scientific work and the obstacles involved in translating bench results into bedside therapies.

But sometimes neither science nor medicine are enough to provide outstanding patient care. The importance of first-rate care had been apparent since my own experience as a young patient, but it was cemented by an experience as a volunteer on the postpartum floor at our local hospital. When a mother lost her baby, a nurse would fix a small card to her door meant to signal the tragic event to the rest of the staff. The card was a picture of a single leaf, perhaps meant to signify the fragility and preciousness of life. A glimpse into the room would reveal a woman who had died a little with her lost child, and I had to learn how to interact with this woman to help care for her.

This often meant just standing by her bedside and asking if there was anything I could do to help her or to make her more comfortable. In this way, I let her know that I would not shy away from her enormous grief and I would do everything in my power to help her to heal. A long day in the lab, a failed experiment, or a year's experiments lost are nothing compared to the pain that will stay with this woman forever. It would not have been enough to offer the usual platitudes and tell her "everything's going to be all right," because it simply wouldn't be. Her doctors must know how to heal her body with techniques developed in labs, while at the same time trying to treat her wounded soul with skills that no laboratory can teach. It is the thought of achieving both of these goals that attracts me most to medicine.

The Family Crisis

M any applicants to medical school have experienced the death of a loved one. In fact, by the time we hit our twenties, most of us have grieved over the loss of a relative. However, people are amazingly resilient; life goes on, and the way a crisis or tragedy affected you can make for a memorable essay.

Be careful, though. This topic is the one that comes with the most warning labels. The essay is not the place to explore the dark recesses of your grief, recite maudlin clichés, or make outlandish claims ("Although I was only four years old when my grandfather died, I decided then that I would devote my life to saving others"). That's not to say that discussing someone's suffering or death and how you handled it is taboo. It can be done, and the essays in this section did it well.

Heather C. Tauschek writes gracefully about her grandmother's breast cancer, and admits with refreshing candor that she "experienced no major changes" during the illness. Her essay weaves poignant specifics with critical issues facing medicine today, and one can see how it would prompt a stimulating interview with an admissions officer. Aasim I. Padela's father had cancer and his aunt attempted suicide, while Jennifer Halverson's thirteen-year-old brother died in an accident, a fact she doesn't even mention until the end of her essay. For Ginny Kullman, it was her mother's breast cancer that convinced her to pursue medicine.

Clearly, all these students were ultimately influenced by the events of their lives. Heather learned how important it was not to make big changes, so that her grandmother could die in dignity, with her family. Aasim was drawn to the dual role of the physician, as counselor and caregiver, while Jennifer gained empathy and an inner strength she didn't know she had. And Ginny mentions her mother's disease and how it relates to her only as a jumping-off point for the rest of her essay.

None of these essays makes the family crisis the focus. But in each of them, the event gave the writer a stronger rationale for choosing medicine. Remember, essays about the loss or critical illness of a loved one are probably the most common. If you have truly been moved to pursue medicine in this manner, be sure to place it squarely in the context of your life, your experience, and your work. Support your claims with evidence from the way you've spent your time in and out of school. After all, an essay about your deep desire to find a cure for breast cancer will look hollow if all you've done is become social chairman of your sorority.

HEATHER C. TAUSCHEK

The pungency of sickness coated with Glade Powder Fresh Blue heavies the air. In the bedroom, a little ball of purple leotard and lavender tulle—my blond, four-year-old sister—curls up between Grandma Tootsie and the sturdy silver rails of the hospital bed. Breast cancer metastasized to bone, and my grandmother now sips nectar through the morphine drip butterflied into her wrist.

My world changes little with Tootsie's cancer. Like always, Sundays are for brunch and Go Fish by the fireplace, I in my pajamas and Tootsie wrapped in a knitted blanket. I play dress-up in Tootsie's clothes, only now they are slit up the back for easy removal. And I still spend the night at her house, but now it is every night and my parents occupy a rumpled mattress on Tootsie's bedroom floor. Then my grandmother fades, blue eyes rolling into her head as her body seizes, slipping into a coma, and a tear traverses her sunken cheek as she hears me say that I love her. One evening, a silent ambulance carries her body from her home, and my mother, father, sisters, and I watch through the window and grieve.

I was young when Tootsie was ill, and, while our lives were adjusted slightly, we experienced no major changes: Tootsie was simply sick and we were helping her. But in retrospect, I understand that such lack of change was exactly what Tootsie's physician wanted, and it was exactly what allowed Tootsie to die with the "dignity" she craved. Rather than sending her to a hospital to die, the physician fought for Tootsie to be one of Alaska's earliest trials of home morphine-infusion pumps, connected my mother and father with hospice nurses, and taught my parents how to care for Tootsie's ailing body—helping her maintain, as much as possible, the life that she loved while acknowledging the painful metamorphosis of her body. Because of this physician's care, my grandmother experienced joy, love, and life in the midst of the process of dying, and it is this type of care I hope to give one day to my own patients.

Tuesday. It is "Seniors Making Art" day at the nursing home near my house, and wheelchairs are pulled close to a circular piece of plywood, the size of a tabletop for six. Mosaic hands, each created by an Alzheimer's patient on a previous day, are glued solidly to the wood, and today we are sorting out translucent grays to fill the cracks between fingers. Spread on butcher paper like water-tumbled stones, small pieces of rainbow-hued glass slide from piles. Some quavering fingers sort colors—gray from red, yellows placed in another bowl— while others dance nervously, moving pieces left to right, right to left, scoot a little with the palm and back, over and over. I, too, run my fingers through rainbow rivers of color, and, somehow, the juxtaposition of colors and the contrast of smooth table against hard-edged glass is soothing. In this place the Alzheimer's patients and I are the same—we simply receive the sensory beauty in prismatic colors or gentle chinking of glass. Like a child stroking a soft ribbon or cats stretching their bellies at dusk on sun-warmed paving stones, such things bring simple, immediate, inexplicable joy and connect us to the surrounding world.

When human biology goes awry, our place in the world is altered. Sometimes personality is affected; at other times the body traps its bearer: Limbs deteriorate, muscles atrophy, or bodies simply age. Sickness is a fissure preventing women, children, or men from filling the community roles that give them dignity and personhood. In many cases, the fissure's walls may be rejoined by pharmaceuticals or the surgeon's knife. But what happens when sickness is terminal, when disease is unfettered by our remedies, when an Alzheimer's patient is a confused vestige of the person who once was?

In these places, healing must become reconciliation: two estranged parties brought into new harmony by home hospice care, creating art, or any other activity that spans the barrier of sickness and restores an individual's community and sense of belonging. As a physician, I hope to be this agent of reconciliation.

AASIM I. PADELA

My initial exposure to the medical field came through the experiences of my father and my aunt as medical patients. It was in Pakistan and in my presence that my aunt attempted to commit suicide. I remember the air of desperation as we tried to keep her conscious and to counter the effects of the poison. The situation drastically changed when the doctor arrived as he instilled a sense of calm and proceeded to attend to my aunt. His caring nature was apparent as he spent the night reassuring my family. In the weeks to come he made many visits to the home, working to repair my aunt's psyche and marriage. Health concerns shook my family again several years later when my father developed cancer. As his condition worsened, I felt increasingly powerless against the rampage of the disease. Once again, it was our doctor who was the harbinger of hope. He mentioned a possible treatment, but being medically uninsured my family could not afford it. We took on extra jobs, asked friends and relatives for financial assistance, and prayed for a solution. Thankfully, the therapy was financed and my father survived his battle with cancer. These two experiences helped me to realize the dual role physicians play as counselors and health care providers, and inspired within me a desire to practice medicine.

While I did shadow local physicians during high school, it was not until college, when I joined the campus medical emergency response team and a local ambulance corps as an emergency medical technician, that I became directly involved in patient care. The experiences have given me a preview of what a medical career entails. Many hours are spent studying about human biology and medical treatment, while even more time is devoted to training. The feelings of excitement as I rush out to meet a patient, and of fulfillment when I know I have done all I could to make a difference in the patient's life, are worth all of the hard work. I look forward to a medical career in which I can play an increased and more significant role in patient care.

It was also in college where I was exposed to the research side of medicine. I have worked on various projects at the University of Rochester Medical Center (URMC), Rochester General Hospital (RGH), and the National Institute of Child Health and Human Development (NICHD), applying biomedical engineering skills to medical research. At RGH I studied leiomyomas and myometrial hyperplasia and their clinical effects, thus aiming to further medical knowledge of uterine complications. My work at URMC and NICHD had a different aim, that of innovating medical technology to be used in clinical diagnosis and monitoring. At URMC, I was involved with the design of an experiment, along with its requisite tools, aimed at using MRI as an early indicator of osteoarthritis, and at NICHD using visible light spectroscopy in biological tissue analysis. I have learned much about medical research and its methods through these experiences, and hope to apply that knowledge in my future career.

My life experiences have steered me toward, and given me a deeper understanding of, the medical field. Balancing a strong academic record with extracurricular interests and employment has helped to shape me into a well-rounded person capable of dealing with the challenges of a medical career. By pursuing biomedical engineering, a foundation for both medical school and future research prospects has already been set. If given the opportunity to enter medical school I will build upon this base and come a step closer to fulfilling my personal and professional goals.

JENNIFER HALVERSON

The screaming of the little boy's mother shattered the relative serenity in the room. The nurse and I quickly ran over to the child's bed. His body had just gone limp in his mother's arms. I maneuvered my way through the crowd of people gathering around the boy and listened for a heartbeat. All I heard were a few faint, irregular thumps. "I barely hear anything," I yelled across the room to the nurse. He brought over two syringes of epinephrine, injecting one into the boy's arm as I continued to monitor his heartbeat. It slowly became stronger and faster but remained irregular. The nurse handed me the second syringe before running off to find the doctor on call for the night. I continued monitoring his heart while trying to comfort his parents until the doctor came. "This child is critically ill," the doctor reported after checking his vitals, "and probably won't live through the night." I wanted to scream in protest. I wanted to believe he would pull through. I left the ward reluctantly that night and returned early the next morning. The doctor was right; the little boy had died during the night. It is likely that he had severe pneumonia, though no "official" cause of death was ever determined. This is the way it is in third-world countries like Haiti, where thousands of children die daily from malnutrition and preventable diseases.

I have been on three humanitarian work trips to Haiti over the past year and will return twice this summer. I watched this boy die and I have watched other children die, but I have also watched many, many children recover from malnutrition, meningitis, tuberculosis, parasites, pneumonia, and other conditions. My experiences in Haiti have allowed me to see two sides of medicine—reality and hope. Medical professionals cannot cure everything; they cannot "play god." Yet they persevere because they have seen people live as a result of their efforts. The faces of the people who survive fill their minds and give them the strength to continue with their work. As each day passed in Haiti, my desire to become a physician intensified as I learned more and more about medicine from several physicians who taught me about the human body, ethics, procedures, and people as we worked together. Cherished memories fill my mind as I anticipate returning there in one week and as I look forward to the possibility of becoming a physician myself.

My love for working with people is not limited to Haiti and is not limited to medicine. I am aware that there are deep needs here in America. My work with Simpson Housing Services' emergency shelter in Minneapolis, where I have volunteered for two years, has opened my eyes to this fact. As a volunteer on the night shift, I register and interact with guests, assist the shelter coordinators, and obtain needed supplies. In addition, I have organized and led several overnight visits to the shelter, including breakfast preparation, for Calvary Church's senior high students.

Volunteering at the shelter gives me the opportunity to relate on an interpersonal level with people from a variety of ethnic and socioeconomic backgrounds. Through our conversations I have learned how to interact and communicate cross-culturally. The many hours I have spent at Simpson have, at different times, been humorous, thought-provoking, tiring, and even frightening. These experiences have given me a desire to work full-time in an urban neighborhood because I am now acutely aware of the need for primary-care physicians in these areas. I want to be one of these physicians.

I have also dealt firsthand with grief and loss. Five years ago, my thirteen-year-old brother died suddenly in a skiing accident. The pain of dealing with this loss for the past five years has taught me to persevere through difficult situations. When I meet people who are dealing with difficult times, I have something to offer them because I truly understand their emotional trials, if only in a small way. This comfort extends to the Haitian family that has just lost a child and to the homeless man who has not seen a family member in years. The reality of the world is that sometimes life is very hard, and we have no choice but to deal with these challenges. But I also believe in hope, and I know that physicians have many opportunities to bring hope to people.

My desire to be a physician extends back to my childhood and has encompassed much thought and exploration. During junior and senior high school, I wrote papers on biomedical research, bone marrow transplants, and human embryo cloning. I shadowed a pediatric oncologist and a neonatologist to learn about the daily work of physicians. I have had a lifelong intrigue with and a long-standing, intense interest in medicine. I believe I have the ability to handle the rigors of medical school and the compassion and humanity to be a very good doctor.

GINNY KULLMAN

My mother was diagnosed with breast cancer when she was thirty and I was three years old. My memory of this time is clouded with tangibles, including wigs, prosthetic breasts, and hospital bracelets; clearly I was unable to grasp the severity of the disease at such a young age. Over time, I became inquisitive about my family's history of cancer and its relation to my Jewish descent. Discovering my strong genetic predisposition to breast cancer sparked my interest to study medicine. The fact that math and science are my academic strengths further inspired me to pursue this career.

Yet how could I confidently assume that I wanted to be a physician with no concept about what a physician's daily routine entailed? My mother is a social worker and my father is an attorney, and none of my relatives in New Orleans are physicians. I dedicated the past four summers to exploring the many facets of medicine in order to gain greater insight. Originally interested in research, I spent three consecutive summers in different laboratories: human genetics, cancer, and neuroscience. This exposure proved to be a valuable learning experience, as I saw the concepts I learned in theory applied in practice. Also, I now appreciate researchers' relentless efforts to endure tedious protocols and hopefully await results. Most importantly, I discovered that I longed for contact with patients.

In an attempt to fill this gap, this summer I shadowed an oncologist at Presbyterian Hospital. I benefited from close patient interaction; I examined malignant breast tumors, observed nurses administer chemotherapy, and aided patients on their deathbed and the stages in between. I also sat in on internal medicine residents' morning report and physician conferences. The overall experience was not demoralizing, but exhilarating and uplifting. I watched and learned from the doctor. He was calm and always sincerely listened to his patients. He gave them hope. "Why pay to go to the movies to see heroes when I can see them every day?" he would routinely state.

To experience different patient populations and specialties, I also observed a pediatrician at Ochsner Hospital. It was immediately evident that pediatricians are faced with an array of different, yet no less important tasks. In this specialty, it is important to communicate with both the sick child and with the mother or father who is in the room. The doctor always listened intently and asked all of the right questions at the appropriate time, serving as both a healer and an advisor.

While my main goal was to observe patient-physician interaction, I was also able to assess the physicians' qualities that allowed them to become accomplished practitioners. I was encouraged by the fact that I, too, possess these traits. Good listening skills are paramount to fostering a trusting rapport with patients and taking their history. I was chosen as a Student Listener in high school and advised troubled or homesick classmates in my dormitory. At the University of North Carolina at Chapel Hill, I was selected to an advising position in my sorority, where I counseled students on a wide range of issues, from class selection to alcohol abuse.

In addition to listening, I understand the self-discipline and perseverance that are equally important to endure the arduous study, long hours, emotional and mental strain, and moral and legal responsibility that are an integral part of the medical student's and eventually the doctor's daily existence. I am not deterred by the prospect of a grueling physical routine or the lack of leisure time. Although I work effectively independently, I know the importance of group participation. The UNC Honors Program has provided me with small, discussion-oriented classes similar to those I profited from at boarding school. These classes allow students to bounce ideas off one another and collectively work to solve problems. These class dynamics are similar to the discussions I observed at morning report with internal medicine residents.

I have always grown up with the prospect of cancer in my future. Yet looking ahead, I see a pathway that leads not to cancer, but to medical school and eventually a career in medicine. I cannot recall a specific time when I chose medicine; instead I would affirm that medicine chose me. I am excited to foster trusting relationships with patients, solve problems, and continue the learning process throughout my career. Physicians often warn me about the challenging career I face, one where the financial rewards have been curbed significantly. I reply that I look forward to accepting the challenge. As for the rewards, they will come every day when I can care for and heal "heroic" patients.

Go Ahead—Make My Day

This is the tough-guy essay. The best examples demonstrate an intellectually curious and disciplined mind that yearns to go one more step. These students, fascinated by the challenges of science and research, take every hard class and want more. Bring it on! They want to increase their own knowledge—and the whole body of scientific knowledge that grows and changes continually. They want challenging cases, and they want to succeed.

The first writer, William Ward, volunteered as an emergency medical technician (as many applicants do). He begins with an anecdote that vividly conveys his infectious enthusiasm. Although he grew up in a family of doctors, he indicates no complacency or sense of entitlement in his piece.

The second writer, Reuben Strayer, was a recruited basketball player and considered trying to play professionally, but he ultimately chose an unusual college major and the more challenging path of medicine.

With a different set of challenges growing up, Khurram Javed was accustomed to overcoming obstacles. He chooses one of the most difficult paths, a combination M.D./Ph.D.

Next, Chloeanne Estrera began as a journalist. Her first challenge was to immerse herself in the best premed program she could find. To do this, she transferred colleges, and she uses her essay to explain the hardships of playing catch-up.

Finally, Chad Roach takes us through the painful experience—literally painful—of learning that "the prize is not in the destination, but in the journey." He draws a connection between the unusual sport of tae kwon do and his commitment to medicine.

73

Medicine is a difficult, demanding path to choose. It requires dedication, intelligence, stamina, and endurance. Students who are excited by the challenges will use a medical career not as a money machine but as a catalyst for progress in their fields. There is nothing static about the science of healing. Medical schools need students who have a passion for research and for learning, students who will be tomorrow's scientists, and students who look at the impossible and decide it just takes a little longer to achieve.

WILLIAM WARD

A call blasted over my fire department pager in the middle of an icy winter night in rural Ohio. "Beep! Beep! Beep! Attention, College Township squad personnel, you have a squad run to an elderly female with difficulty breathing and a history of heart disease." I jumped from my dorm room bed, raced to the firehouse, and boarded the departing ambulance. Though it was far from being my first run, I did not yet feel like a veteran EMT, and I buzzed with excitement as our crew hurried to the scene. As we approached the house, an icy patch sent our ambulance squarely into the roadside ditch—hopelessly stuck. The senior officers had to radio for help, which left me in charge of going to the house and directing patient care for the first time. I was eager to take the responsibility, which I had acted through in my head so many times, and my mind raced even faster than my feet as I stepped through the doorway. The patient lay on her couch, and she gave me a look of relief as I knelt beside her, taking her hand as a comforting gesture. I introduced myself and listened carefully to her medical history. I concentrated on her vital signs and EKG for guidance in tailoring my questions and subsequent treatments. In the hour it took to get the ambulance back on the road I got to know my patient and hopefully made her feel more comfortable. I believe that I not only did my job well, but that I made a real connection with the patient.

Since that night almost two years ago, I have had hundreds more opportunities to direct patient care and help people as an EMT. Not every experience has been as memorable, but from each patient I care for I learn new things. The myriad diseases, medications, and injuries that I encounter have consistently piqued my curiosity and prompted me to seek more information. I have learned to use the scientific literature and my parents' expert advice as doctors to help me understand interesting and challenging topics in my work as an EMT.

My ambitions have reached beyond emergency medicine into investigating broader topics in medicine and health care and applying what I learn to efforts for the health of the community. For the past year I have worked with the campus physician and the Student Medical Advisory Committee to start a campaign aimed at banning smoking in all college buildings and providing support to students who want to stop smoking. Also, every Sunday I host a medical information program on the college radio station. To prepare for the show, I research a broad range of topics within current medical news, technology, and health care. The radio show has challenged me to think carefully about sensitive and difficult topics, and discussions with callers have prompted me to look at issues from new perspectives. I believe that keeping abreast of medical developments and researching topics in emergency medicine have helped me contribute both to the health of my college and to my skills for treating patients.

When investigating topics in medicine, I use many of the skills that I have learned as a student researcher in biology. Over the past three school years and two summers I have worked closely with professors as a Kenyon Summer Science Scholar and Biology Honors Scholar. In my research I have focused on topics ranging from the molecular biology of drosophila to my Senior Honors project on the behavioral ecology of barnacles. The knowledge I have gained, the ability to interpret, write, and apply scientific literature, and my familiarity with the scientific method should be valuable tools for studying medicine.

In summary, I have discovered my interest in science and medicine through my work as a student researcher, through the rewards of volunteering as an emergency medical technician, and as a college health activist. I grew up in a family of physicians. Over the past three years I have worked closely with doctors, nurses, and paramedics through my training and practice as an EMT-Basic and then as an EMT-Intermediate. Those experiences, as well as weeks spent learning from doctors in the operating room and the emergency room, have shown me the considerable commitment, strain, and difficulty confronted by people, especially physicians, at various places in the medical system. However, I have seen that with the challenges physicians face, there also come rewards. I have discovered how interesting, enlightening, and enjoyable learning about and practicing medicine can be, and it excites me to think about the lifelong challenges I will face as a physician.

REUBEN STRAYER

I have been drawn to medicine ever since my father checked my ears for infections and prescribed medications for me at a young age. As I matured, I challenged the sincerity of these ambitions by questioning whether my ostensible goals arose from within me, or if they were merely the result of being raised in a doctor's family. It has become clear that it does not matter—my intentions are genuine, and a predisposition to pursue medicine does not diminish their validity.

I first confronted this ambition during my senior year in high school when I evaluated the most important passion in my life, basketball. Having represented my school for six years with varying degrees of success, I was recruited by several small colleges, and when it came time for me to apply, I looked at the road ahead and saw two diverging paths: I could either continue to make basketball my first priority or allow my other interests to prevail. It was then that I decided that my mind would take me further than my jump shot, and chose a school that offered an inexhaustible array of academic and extracurricular pursuits. I am comfortable with that decision not only because I have taken advantage of many of those programs but because I can satisfy my lasting hunger for the sport—I continue to play nearly every day and have competed on over a dozen intramural teams, including one intramural champion, worked as a basketball official, and have held both assistant and head coaching positions at a local elementary school. And though the transition from a serious basketball player to a recreational one continues to be difficult, it is through basketball that I keep physically fit (essential to my mental fitness) and relieve the stress of a premedical curriculum. It is through competitive athletics that the principles of practice, perseverance, and often humility have been impressed upon me, and they serve me well—running wind sprints until you pass out on the gymnasium floor generates a certain appreciation for one's capabilities that seems to surface during the last hours of an all-night study session.

Among the most appealing aspects of a career in medicine is the promise of continuous challenge. When I don't test my aptitude and resources I feel stale and impotent, so I have sought challenge in all my pursuits, and strive to assure myself of ample challenge in the future—a career in medicine is the most important means to that end. It has been necessary for me to work part-time since I arrived at college, and through the work-study program I was fortunate enough to land a clerical job that paid well. I stayed with that job for two years because of the salary but noticed that I looked for reasons not to go to work and dreaded the time I spent working.

Toward the end of my second year at school, I searched for a more rewarding job and found one at the campus computer store. At the MicroCenter I am paid a little more than half of my old salary for much more demanding work, but as technical support staff I am confronted with problem after problem for which customers rely on me to find solution after solution. It is the same quest for challenge that "ignited" my interest in motorcycle mechanics and my current training as a motorcycle repair technician. Computer consulting and motorcycle repair entail precise and methodical application of knowledge and diagnostic technique to probe a system for problems and develop solutions. Both of these ambitions as well as basketball allow me to better understand myself by testing my limits and force me to define myself through the continued exercise of my abilities. A career in medicine entails an apprehension of a constantly changing body of knowledge and a continual reunderstanding of the issues, promising the challenge that excites me.

What separates medicine from fixing computers and motorcycles is that the goal of medical science and clinical medicine is to assuage human suffering. As I have grown older, I have come to understand that most are not blessed with a life as comfortable, happy, and healthy as mine. Accordingly, I am driven to pursue a career where I may provide for a world that has generously provided for me. Though the qualities of independence and self-reliance are valuable and fashionable, it is the existence of and interaction with others that endows life with meaning—we are hopelessly social animals. This conclusion partially motivated my change in major from electrical engineering to philosophy. Though I have always had a special fascination with computers, their mechanical, tirelessly predictable nature precludes any sensual satisfaction in their design and application. Philosophy is the charming contrast—wonderfully impractical, stimulating only through argument, so essentially human! It is the inherent interaction, creativity, artistry—the inherent humanity of philosophy—that attracts me. It is the same attraction that compels me to pursue medicine.

The pursuit of medicine demands an awe of the human body that I developed one summer removing femurs and spines from cadavers for orthopedic research, and it demands respect for and appreciation of human suffering. I am intimately familiar with the physical and emotional consequences of illness through the care of a very sick younger sister and through working with patients who have suffered neurological trauma at a local hospital. Most importantly, medicine demands a drive to heal, the seeds of which were planted by my father and have blossomed into an impassioned energy. It is for the above reasons that I feel prepared and excited to channel that energy and dedicate my life to the pursuit of a career in medicine.

KHURRAM JAVED

Passing the corner of a church, I see my building, tall and dark against the night sky. Figures huddle at the entrance. I fight the fear, the instinct to stay away, and keep walking toward home. Their eyes are fixed on me. I ignore their taunts; I'm just here to see my mom. As I walk into the project, I remember an acquaintance from another project who accidentally stepped on someone's shoe. The next day, his front door was riddled with gunfire. This environment allows no margin of error. I was only eleven when I moved there permanently, but even then I grasped the waste of human potential and the resulting misery, and I became determined to use my own potential fully. I steeled myself to the threats, the human filth, and the suffocating violence. I got straight A's in school, although the fact that I went to school made me an object of derision. I knew I wanted to use my abilities in an environment that was the opposite of the projects, one where people care and show compassion. In college, I decided to become a physician and research scientist, not only because this path best utilizes my abilities, but also because it combines creative, disciplined experimentation with helping people.

It was a youthful passion for experiment that fueled my ambition. As a child I moved every year, and this passion provided needed continuity. For example, I loved to build and creatively modify remote-control cars. Once, for a race, I built a "super car." To increase its speed, I doubled both the amount of volts to the motor and the diameter of the tires. I remember the crowd cheering as my car took the lead—and then laughing as the tires popped off and the car caught fire. Through experiments I explored the natural world, astonished at its beauty. In college, I sought out opportunities to do research as I gained sophistication as a scientist. I became involved in several projects in my lab, where I am acquiring a better understanding of the development of the retina. My exposure to high-level science has only strengthened my love of experimentation and further stimulated my imagination. I am completely at home in the lab.

I had not gone to doctors much as a child, and so at college I explored the world of medicine, volunteering at the university hospital's emergency room. Seeing the application of procedures derived from research was illuminating. I realized that working with patients refines a researcher's focus and reveals unexpected considerations. I also saw the desire and motivation of doctors to help people. I felt that desire and motivation, and soon moved beyond tasks such as transferring samples and targeting patients for clinical studies to helping and comforting patients. One was a ninety-one-year-old woman who had suffered a stroke. When I went to speak to her and hold her hand, I was startled to feel how cold she was. As her family members stood around her, crying, her heart started to beat erratically. The doctors rushed over, and I stepped aside. I went home around 2 A.M., depressed. But later, I realized that I was upset because I could not do more for the patient and because there were limits to what medicine could do. Ultimately, this experience, although painful, moved me. It made me want to help individual patients as well to help expand the limits of the possible through research.

My lab and hospital experiences lead me to view clinical practice and research as a continuum. Researchers work to help humanity on the global level and almost never get the chance to see the results in the particular. Physicians work with individual people. I aim to work at both levels and combine globalization with particularization. Volunteering in the clinical environment, I found that I have the sensitivity and personal concern for patients needed to be a complete physician. I had long come to feel there was no way I could *not* do research—it is what sustains me. Now, I see that there is no way I could *not* be a medical doctor, because helping patients fulfills the cycle of healing propelled by the lab, and also fulfills me. For these reasons, I am choosing to enter an M.D./Ph.D. program. I believe that my work in the lab will make me a better clinician and my work with patients will make me a better scholar/scientist. In this dual role, I can bring the reality of individual patients, each with a unique medical personality, into the lab, and the excitement and optimism of research to my patients.

Seeing the waste of human potential in the projects and the resulting misery has made me determined to do everything I can to ease suffering. My struggle to overcome that environment has forced me to develop the stamina, determination, and discipline to aim high and reach my target. Earning an M.D./Ph.D. will be hard, and I embrace the challenge. For physicians and research scientists, there is little margin for error. I am used to that.

CHLOEANNE BOMPAT ESTRERA

Scientist. Artist. Healer.

My decision to become a physician manifested itself in a roundabout way. For the majority of my college career, my academic and extracurricular pursuits lay in journalism, basic sciences, and volunteer work. However multifaceted these interests are, they fit like puzzle pieces to form one picture of one of my strongest goals yet.

My career search began as soon as I enrolled at Boston University, a fast-paced metropolitan institution amidst traffic and cold. Journalism soon became integral to life at BU. The excitement, effort, and long nights meeting deadlines and constructing articles for the college paper fulfilled me, if only temporarily. My other interests at BU later took precedence. They included an advanced chemistry class, which worked like a physical chemistry course. Through it, I developed my abilities as a laboratory chemist. A science disciple since high school, I also wrote about science on a weekly basis for the BU student paper. Chemistry bred the academic scientist in me, and science journalism, the curious artist.

Journalism required me to interact with an array of people. Interviews for articles educated me in conversing with strangers and in learning from them and their life experiences. The human element was essential to each of my articles. One of my main concerns, however, was that news events often left me on the outside. My report, such as a feature story on a physician or a researcher, was only a report. My role in the story itself was indirect and subtle. I wanted to do more than to observe. I wanted to do. The process of researching and writing about the work of scientists, researchers, teachers, and health professionals helped me learn so much about their careers that I decided journalism was not right for me. A career in science and medicine seemed a more optimal fit.

My ambition and talent have grown stronger since freshman year. I transferred from BU to Duke University, where there existed a richer resource of undergraduate exposure to science and medical professions. My start was rough, as you may observe in my academic record. I fell ill during the first summer session of organic chemistry. My illness affected my grade, but I was able to recover and improve in class later on. Determined to master the material, I took the course again. My first physics course, on the other hand, was a struggle, because it was a technical, rather than general, class. I took the general physics course the next semester and did my best.

After sorting through these situations, my record and inner determination to improve it still remained strong. The transfer process was academically and emotionally challenging, but it also helped me hold tight to what I loved to do. The fact that my research in brain cancer treatment could improve lives encouraged me to continue studying drug-polymer carriers, resulting in a senior thesis that earned me a graduation with distinction. In addition, upper-level science courses, ongoing research, and the opportunity to affect and be affected positively by the lives of people I barely knew transformed my college career. I joined a community-service-based fraternity called Alpha Phi Omega and, through it, participated in many service projects and developed leadership skills. I also volunteered at the local hospital, and I continue to work with service groups in the community today. While I was participating in a health care internship at Duke Hospital, several health professionals there allowed me a peek into their daily lives. The interviewing skills I developed as a journalist helped me to develop confidence when talking to patients and their friends and families. The people who would spend nights with bedridden friends or relatives taught me just as much about medicine as the professionals themselves did.

In order to make sure health care was a realistic choice, I continued to volunteer in the medical field. While training to be an emergency medical technician, I explored family medicine by observing a family practice physician for one summer. This physician became my mentor. He was more concerned with the psychological and physical well-being of his patients than with fixing them up and sending them out. In order to heal his patients more effectively, he became an active part of the local community. Through his actions, he taught me to appreciate people and the art of healing them.

By harnessing my scientific tendencies with my desire to heal, I realize my potential to flourish in medicine. I also realize that being a doctor is how I want to live my life. I am nurturing what I have become so far—a scientist, an artist, and a part of a community—into one dream I can pursue with zest and dedication.

CHAD ROACH

I was only six. I remember it like it was yesterday. My favorite Christmas present that year was a microscope. Of course, being six, I really had no idea what it was except that it was making blood big. Not the most appropriate gift for a six-year-old, but Mom was glad to give us whatever the Salvation Army gave her. On the 27th, there was a knock on our door. My mom answered and a minute later came into the family room and said, "Son, I need your microscope." You see, the microscope had been donated by mistake. She took it and left the room. When she came back empty-handed a minute later, I had a puzzled look on my face. She had a tear on hers. "Son, I have to tell you something about Santa Claus."

I was twenty-four. I remember it like it was yesterday. It was the Olympic year and for the first time tae kwon do was slated as a full medal sport. I had trained intensely for eight years for my shot at an Olympic berth, and the next stage of the Olympic Qualifications was only three weeks away. I had already trained physically for six hours that day, and it was time for my nightly stretch and meditation. I warmed up and began my stretch. A few minutes into the routine, I felt the tear. I iced it immediately. I was optimistic. I had five or six other muscles strains at the time—what was one more? Besides, it was hardly painful, certainly not enough to hold me back—not three weeks from the Olympic Qualifier. The next morning I hit the track, and ran four miles and some sprints. Then during my water break, the pain finally hit. Now, it was excruciating, but somehow I managed to hobble home for ice and ibuprofen. It hurt to walk for a whole week. I still competed in the Olympic Qualifier, but could only kick with one leg and was no match for the people who could kick with two. And that was it—my dream was over. All the blood, the sweat, the tears, the fears, the eight years of training, the Friday nights spent kicking instead of dating, at the gym instead of at the party, came down to one easy match my body wouldn't let me win. I had trained six hours a day, six days a week in the two years leading up to the qualifier, sacrificing my grades, finances, and body. Now, instead of the exhilarating climax I had dreamed, my reality was empty and numb. I got on the plane the next day, with a frown still on my face. I buckled up and began flipping through my notebook, looking for solace in my pages of inspirational quotes and proverbs. Shortly, I came upon one of my favorites. It was appropriate: "The prize is not in the destination, but in the journey." I smiled.

I was twenty-six. I remember it like it was yesterday. It was fall and I was just starting medical school. I woke up early that day—my favorite day of that first year. It was the day I got my microscope back and embarked on another incredible journey.

When people hear about my tae kwon do journey, they usually assume the reason I took it is that I love beating people up. It's not. My favorite aspect of the sport is its unique potential as a vehicle for transforming lives. I met Katie when she was eight years old. She had long rusty hair and was shy, dyslexic, and labeled with ADD. When I met her, she couldn't walk in a straight line. She hadn't smiled in years. Her desperate mother enrolled her in tae kwon do on her doctor's recommendation. Mom introduced me to her. "Hi, Katie," I said. No response. She clung to Mom's leg with both arms. "Come try it. It's fun!" No response. My coaxing continued, but to no avail. She was too petrified to move. It took weeks to finally coerce her into participating. Her mother was shocked when five months later, after practicing very hard, Katie earned her yellow belt. When my students were invited to demonstrate at a church, Katie volunteered to go! When it was her turn to perform, she walked up to the board (in a straight line!), and with a loud yell, she kicked and broke it. When she turned around she had a big smile on her face! Her mom had a tear on hers. The joy I have received from helping Katie and others to smile and become happier and more confident has fueled my desire to pursue medicine as a vehicle for transforming lives and making people healthier.

My experiences as a CNA [certified nursing assistant] have also furthered my commitment to medicine. I learned firsthand about the emotional and spiritual aspects of health care. I was exposed to death, despair, and hope, and was called upon by many patients for support. After observing patients interact with other nurses and myself, I concluded that one of the most vital skills in developing rapport and trust with a patient is the ability to listen. I am interviewing next week for several internships in Clinical Pastoral Education, an experience I hope will improve my listening and counseling skills, and help me to become more sensitive to the spiritual and emotional health of patients and the humanistic side of medicine. I have loved people for as long as I can remember. I have also loved science for as long as I can remember. I am excited to merge both passions by studying medicine.

My grades over the last two years are not an indication of my potential, or of my ability to succeed in a university. Rather, they are an indicator of the time I spent in pursuit of other goals. My MCAT scores are more indicative of my ability. My course load has been heavy, and I have worked all four years, often full-time. This was in addition to the hours I spent training for the Olympics. During my summers, I enjoy volunteering with the Special Olympics, WEAVE (Women Escaping a Violent Environment), and other groups, and teaching children's and women's awareness classes to day cares and community groups. My life philosophy: Every moment is special. My teaching philosophy: Lead by example.

Turning Points

H ow do you use your experiences to change and grow? The "turning point" essay can show how thoughtful and responsive you are—and how you handle a stressful situation.

One incident rarely changes a person's life. Trying to persuade a reader that a single event suddenly revolutionized your perspective on Life, the Universe, and Everything is likely to sound (and be) contrived rather than profound. Nevertheless, discussing a specific experience can be a great way to express the evolution of a change that developed over time.

The mistake made most often in "turning point" essays is the assumption that it must involve a Major Event or a Big Lesson. Not so. While you can't tell your life story in the confines of an application essay, you can show an important piece of yourself through a detailed examination of a key moment in your life. Think of the moments as pieces of a mosaic; each one may be small, but the absence of one piece destroys the beauty of the whole.

To become a doctor requires enormous commitment and sacrifice. Just the decision to apply to med school isn't easy. By focusing on one aspect of your journey, you can use your essay to illustrate how the pieces all came together.

The first writer in this section experienced the death of a patient before he ever applied to medical school. It made him think carefully about what being a doctor is really all about. He artfully combines that experience with his scientific accomplishments and study abroad to create a fine essay.

Neesha Amin shadowed a doctor who had to tell a patient that her cancer was no longer in remission. She emphasizes that her multicultural heritage gives her an advantage when dealing with a wide variety of patients. Neesha uses an expressive image when she writes, "The tumor had resurfaced like a lie of the past coming back to haunt you."

The next applicant writes about his painful determination to achieve competence in playing the sitar, and then relates the musical image to his experience with an AIDS patient. Paul Mullan's injury to his hand while playing baseball and his work in the ER allowed him to observe the power doctors have to heal both physical and spiritual wounds. And Brian Brunson also follows a trail of personal injuries and hospital work to illustrate his path to orthopedics.

Finally, Lawrence J. Young was inspired by a brutal attack from a troubled teen he was counseling. Lawrence is a nontraditional applicant: At age thirty-one, after establishing a career as a mental health counselor, he decided to get his M.D. As his essay reveals, what the attack taught him about himself became the pivotal moment in his decision.

There are all types of changes that occur in your life. By choosing one of them to examine very closely, you may write an outstanding essay—and learn something about yourself in the process.

NAME WITHHELD

M s. "G" was really wearing my patience thin.

For the past twenty minutes in her hospital room, I had been trying to convince the small, elderly woman to enroll in a clinical research project. Although I had repeatedly explained that having five milliliters of blood drawn right after her upcoming surgery would not harm her, Ms. G still adamantly refused to participate. Finally, her daughter, who was sitting next to Ms. G's bed, gently smiled and told her agitated mother that there was nothing to fear and that the project would only help doctors improve future surgeries. Even though Ms. G glared at me suspiciously as she signed informed-consent papers, I was relieved that her daughter had been able to calm her.

The next day, when I went to the intensive care unit to see Ms. G after her open-heart procedure, I was shocked to see a crowd of concerned doctors around her bed trying to resuscitate her. While I watched one doctor's hands repeatedly push down on her frail chest, a nurse explained to me that an emergency "code blue" effort was attempting to save her life. As I left the unit, I felt a mix of hope and regret—hope that Ms. G would survive her complications, but regret that I had not been more understanding of her fears a day earlier. The hope disappeared and the regrets amplified when I came back to the ICU later and found that her bed had been removed.

I still wish that I could somehow apologize to Ms. G for my impatience with her the day before she died. Yet the unfortunate incident last summer made clear to me what compassion really is. While I had focused on rationally convincing Ms. G that having five milliliters of blood drawn after her surgery would not harm her, I had not consoled her fears concerning the unknown outcome of the upcoming surgery itself. Indeed, her daughter's warm smile and heartfelt words not only comforted Ms. G during what turned out to be her final hours but have inspired me to relate to those suffering with as much emotional support as possible.

As a clinical research assistant at Methodist Hospital in my hometown, I spent most of last summer talking one-on-one with heart-surgery patients such as Ms. G. Interestingly, I have spent most of this past academic year engaged in one-on-one interactions as well, albeit in a completely different environment—that is, the private tutorial system at Oxford University in England. While conversations at Methodist Hospital nurtured my desire for sharing compassion, personal tutorials at Oxford have developed my capability for critical thought.

I was initially surprised when my first private tutor at Oxford told me that our bioenergetics course would have no proper textbook. Although I had enjoyed and done well in my first two years of lecture classes at Emory University, I soon learned that to compare different books and journal articles on my own successfully I had to think more critically about my readings. In evaluating the relative reliability of my sources before my tutorials, I even discovered errors in the introductory biochemistry textbook I had trusted at Emory. Having discussed my assessments of topics such as magnetic resonance imaging and X-ray diffraction with Oxford professors, I believe that my efforts toward a complete, accurate understanding of such subjects have enhanced my intellectual judgment.

Yet a personal improvement in critical thinking has not been my only gain from a year in England. Although I was very much a part of Emory's campus life during my freshman and sophomore years, my time abroad has truly shown me how much working as part of a community can accomplish, no matter how small or large that community may be. While rowing down the Thames River as a member of a novice crew, I have felt the extra speed that a boat picks up when all eight rowers learn to stroke together in perfect rhythm. In volunteering at the Oxford Night Shelter, I have seen how a team of helpers spending their Saturday morning making sandwiches can treat all the homeless people in a city out to lunch for a day. And, although my earlier research at Emory and at Methodist Hospital had resulted in publications, my work at the Oxford Laboratory of Molecular Biophysics has shown me the added power of working in a scientific community of global scale. Crystals I have grown of a phosphorylase purified by our group's collaborators in Italy were recently diffracted by a synchrotron X ray in France, and the international effort may result in a structure.

During my senior year, I want to bring my refreshed senses of compassion and critical thought back to my peers on Emory's campus and to my honors project, respectively. But in the long run, I believe that these qualities will provide the foundation for a career as a physician-scientist, and I hope to become a strong part of the academic medical community.

NEESHA AMIN

"The cancer is no longer in remission. I am very sorry," said Dr. Montoya as he gently placed his hand on the patient's shoulder. As I stood in the back of the patient's examining room, those words echoed through my head and a piercing pain enveloped my heart. It's back, I thought, after all those weeks of chemotherapy and radiation, just when she had thought things were finally getting better. The tumor had resurfaced like a lie of the past coming back to haunt you. As the reality of the situation became clear, her tears began to flow, and the pain that was once in my heart began to creep slowly through my chest and into my throat. I could feel her pain—it was so real. I clenched my teeth and fought hard to hold back my own tears.

I was shadowing Dr. Montoya that summer to gain a realistic viewpoint of what it is like to be a physician, and my experience that morning proved to be as real as it gets. That night, I wrestled with fears of whether or not I was capable of handling the challenges of a career in medicine. I thought that my being on the verge of crying in that patient's room was a sign of weakness. What I realized very soon, though, was that this seeming "weakness" was really at the heart of why I wanted to practice medicine. My feelings were not a sign of frailty but rather a reflection of something wonderful—the making of a human connection. The ability to do this on a regular basis is one of the most powerful yet overlooked attributes of a physician and it is in this realm that I have a unique advantage. Being born in the United Kingdom, growing up in Africa, and being the child of Indian parents has allowed me to go past tolerating the differences in people. I actually understand them. I have lived in a country where the ailing and impoverished children were not on TV but practically in my back-yard. Where the medical system was so behind that my mother had to fly to the United Kingdom just to give birth. So when I was volunteering and a child would come in sick due to neglect, I would understand where he was coming from. Because I am a product of so many different cultures, I have pieces of each within myself, like a patchwork quilt sewn over many years. As an aspiring physician, I can draw upon these patches whenever I have to deal with a new face or situation.

In addition to my love for making connections with people is my passion for learning. To me, an ideal physician embodies this duality of objectivity and humanity. I have always been the type of person that asks why or how something works and I have loved school since I have been old enough to attend. My mother always tells me a story of when I was in my first year of school. Our family had planned a trip to Victoria Falls, but I refused to go because I simply did not want to miss any days of school. This from a five-year-old child. My ultimate desire to be a physician is driven by my inner self. Just as my personality is twofold, a balance between a genuine interest in people as well as the science of healing, so is the art of medicine.

It was only during the summer that I shadowed Dr. Montoya that I began to truly understand what it means not just to practice medicine but to do it with such grace. Dr. Montoya remained coolly objective yet compassionate, and as he explained to Ms. Brown the regimen of chemotherapy that would begin next week, I slowly made my way to the front of the room. I offered her a glass of water and a smile. What could I possibly say? How could I even begin to articulate what I felt? I held her hand, and just as Dr. Montoya finished and the first second of silence was upon us, I whispered, "I'll be here next week." That said it all.

NAME WITHHELD

For some time now, I have had to endure teeth-clenching pain on a weekly basis. Every week, I attend a sitar lesson, during which I force myself to play my raga even as the instrument's metal strings dig painfully into my fingers causing them to bleed. I try to concentrate since every mistake means starting all over. My teacher, a sarod maestro, insists that he has undergone far harsher training at the hands of his grandfather. I sometimes wonder if the pain is worth it. In the end, though, when my cuts callus, I am able to look past the pain and struggle and become lost in the beauty of my ragas.

The struggle of mastering an instrument has never overshadowed the joy of finally creating music. By applying the same passion, patience, and discipline that I have for music, I hope to master a finer art form—medicine. The path to medicine will likely be difficult and, at times, tiresome. Yet, I find joy in struggles that lead to a positive end. On two separate occasions, I have seen the beauty that the art of medicine can create. Each time, it threatened to forever intoxicate me, beckoning me to follow and neglect the pain and struggle along the way.

The first occasion happened in an old, battered building typical of Chicago's public-housing system: a fourteen-story box with boarded windows, dim lighting, leaky plumbing, and thread-hung elevators. My mission there was simple: deliver a paper bag full of hot meals for a man living with AIDS. I pushed the button for the elevator with my bandaged finger; my knife had slipped the day before while preparing the hot meals I carried that afternoon. Getting off on the tenth floor, I knocked gently on his door. The man who opened it seemed quite healthy. I silently handed him the food and was about to leave when the look in his eyes stopped me. There, the pain and suffering of fighting his horrible disease were apparent. I decided to start a conversation, and suddenly, his eyes brightened as a smile swept across his face. His misery momentarily disappeared. The gratification received from that moment, from the beauty of his disease-transcending smile, felt like the cadence of a beautiful symphony.

What caused that moment, however, was not simply my effort to ease his life. His ability to answer the door, talk with me, and smile brightly was the result of medications discovered by medical scientists who struggle in laboratories, examine his disease, and look for its treatment. The second occasion was interning in research at various medical laboratories. There, I have learned the rewards of becoming a physician who translates advances in medical research into clinical practice. The inherently laborious work in laboratories—the days spent learning to use a flow cytometer, the weeks spent troubleshooting a PCR reaction, and the months spent developing a drug-delivery system for a rat's brain—is worth the final result obtained after years of research: a more melodious life for our family, friends, and fellow human beings.

To the end of including research in my career, I will begin graduate study at Oxford University this fall, having been accepted to study neuroscience in the Department of Physiology. I have a particular fondness for this area due to past experience doing research in the field, a taste for the computational aspects of the brain, and an interest in advancing a medical field that offers much diagnosis but little treatment. I have always planned to earn a doctorate to complement my medical education and will take advantage of that opportunity at Oxford if I can establish a workable thesis proposal by next spring. Eventually, I hope to become an academic physician, integrating research and teaching with patient care.

In my life's pursuits for the highest virtues of art, beauty, and truth, I find one road leading toward community service and another toward science. At the intersection lies the art of medicine. Mastering this art requires one to struggle through various emotional and physical obstacles. However, for the beauty such as that embodied by the AIDS victim's smile, the struggle is worth it. Let the raga begin.

PAUL MULLAN

Seconds after my unbalanced Nolan Ryan windup, all I could feel was my thumb, twisted into an unfamiliar shape. Several terrifying minutes passed until I was in the ER, with a doctor and his medical student examining my hand. I do not remember the questions he asked, nor the setting of the cast, but I do clearly recall leaving that hospital aware that there are opportunities to learn how to restore both the injured physical part and the wounded spirit of another person. Since that first pitch, I have gradually come to realize my aspirations to become a doctor.

Eager to discover this unknown world, I later began volunteering in the outpatient ward, offering a hand to patients recovering from surgery. By walking a fatigued patient to use the bathroom, feeding soup to an incapable woman, or even assisting a nurse, I wanted to make people feel comfortable. After a doctor's encouragement, at age sixteen, I trained for my EMT certification, and soon started to volunteer for the late-night spot in the ER of D.C. General Hospital. Although I had been to the ER for my infamous fastball, a pencil that pierced my hand, and a lathe that had sliced into my pinkie finger, none of these incidents prepared me for my first week in this ER. A gunshot wound was the first code I witnessed, and my responsibility was to run the hallways to the blood bank to replenish the victim's diminishing blood supply. By my third run for another unit of blood, the doctors had called the time of death, and the medical students and I examined the opened chest of this young man. The ER environment demanded endurance and dedication by all of its workers. The amount I learned and experienced in the ER each night became addictive, and after talking with some paramedics, I was hired onto an ambulance unit starting after high school.

I knew that my active role had a tangible impact on the healthy outcome of another person's life during a car wreck I had witnessed. I managed the accident by calming the hysterical driver, stabilizing his neck, and directing other bystanders to divert traffic until the 911 unit arrived. Most patients I handled on the ambulance needed transport between hospitals for a specific operation. The grasp of a warm hand and soft words of encouragement helped to comfort patients and stabilize their vital signs on the way to an otherwise traumatic event. I was the most satisfied after alleviating the grief of a girl my age with a possible ectopic pregnancy; I could not imagine the fear she was experiencing, but I managed to raise her hopes on the ride to the hospital with words of assurance and hope. This ability to work closely with patients made me well prepared for my upcoming position on a clinical research team, volunteering my nights at the Lincoln Hospital ER in the South Bronx.

Initially, the challenge of obtaining personal information from patients who were both older and from a different background than myself was intimidating; however, I was again surprised at the overwhelming effects of sitting next to a person, offering them a friendly handshake, and simply listening to their needs. This program offered the dual benefit of both caring on the local level and offering future benefits for patients elsewhere. The excitement involved in pioneering a new field attracted me into lab research, where I sought to manipulate the gene for collagenase, an enzyme responsible for arthritic diseases. The project culminated in a presentation at Cornell Medical School in front of doctors and researchers. Research gave me a greater appreciation for the endless hours invested to produce one sentence in a science textbook.

However, in my undergraduate science lectures, I was disappointed by the lack of contact and cooperation between students and professors. Therefore, I became a teacher who fostered the positive student interaction necessary to produce accomplished students. I have taught science to seventh-graders in Harlem, tutored adults for their G.E.D., and now I am teaching literacy to youths in a dual language program at P.S. 145. Many of the younger students in these classes come from broken homes and lack a positive role model in their lives. Therefore I stress not only the standards of sentence structure but also such fundamentals as eye contact and a confident handshake. My fascination with teaching soon led me to become a T.A. for the Columbia biology course. I knew that each student in my section had the ability to do well, and I sought to motivate them in this tough course via constant communication and an active learning environment, and encouraged them to venture beyond the classroom level. My favorite moment occurred when the professor posted the study guide I had written on how to succeed in the course.

The skills and tools that I have acquired through my experiences will help me instruct my patients on how to effectively manage and prevent their ailments. In college, I have expanded outside the secure lecture halls and libraries. In research, I have fed my intellectual hunger both in the lab and at the hospital beds. The community has taught me as much about interpersonal skills as I have taught them in their respective needs. My voyage thus far has served to solidify my initial desires to become a doctor and has further inspired me to excel in the field of medicine.

BRIAN BRUNSON

F ear and uncertainty enveloped my mind as I, a normally happy
thirteen-year-old, sat in the emergency room. Both of my wrists
were likely broken. The right arm, though, was the one causing most
of my distress. Just looking at it upset my stomach and caused me to
wonder what would happen next. I was active in sports, and summer
had just begun; now I was facing possible surgery or even the fact that
my right wrist might require months of rehabilitation. I not only
needed a skilled orthopedic surgeon, but one who was compassionate
and encouraging. The surgeon on call that night provided just that.
He placed as much emphasis on repairing my injuries as he did on offering encouragement throughout the whole ordeal, allowing me to
stay positive over the entire summer as I slowly advanced toward a
full recovery.

The experiences provided by this injury along with a major ankle
injury in high school first introduced me to the field of orthopedics
and a career in medicine. Over the years, a number of varied experiences, in addition to the injuries, have served to entice me further
toward a career in medicine; this includes working directly with patients in a hospital and immersing myself in the biomedical sciences
curriculum at Auburn University. Together, these experiences have
fueled my passion for a career in medicine that will present me the
amazing opportunity to better the human existence.

When I first began attending Auburn, I felt in my heart that a career in medicine was the right path for my life. I just lacked practical
experiences to support my passions. Although my strong performance
in freshman chemistry and biology were indeed encouraging, I needed
the opportunity to work with people. That opportunity came during

the summer in Birmingham, Alabama, where I worked as a patient-care associate whose primary responsibility was to assist the nurses in the care of the patients' needs. It was an extremely valuable experience. I not only gained an appreciation for the work of nurses, but I was also able to work with patients and doctors firsthand. I even observed a few surgeries, including an open-heart bypass procedure. The experience that summer was pivotal in my career pursuits, for it assured me that I had a genuine passion for the field of medicine and the opportunities it presents. Since that summer, my experiences have only served to increase my passion for medicine.

During the summer prior to my junior year, I had the privilege of taking the Hospital Experience course through the College of Sciences and Mathematics and East Alabama Medical Center. In this class, I was able to spend a few hours per week for eight weeks with doctors from eight different specialties. This experience gave me greater understanding and insight into the different career paths for a physician. I learned a great deal about myself that summer. I realized that surgery probably was not the right path for me but that primary care interests me greatly. I was also introduced to the very intriguing field of radiation oncology. Had I not taken this course, I might never have grasped the unique challenges and rewards associated with this field of medicine.

Finally, my educational and community experiences at Auburn have only served to encourage me further toward my goal of becoming a doctor. I have continued to excel in all science and medical-related classes throughout my second and third years at Auburn. The classes I have taken with direct medical applications include vertebrate development, histology, microbiology, genetics, and medical ethics. Not only have I done well in these classes, but they have also been very interesting. In addition, I have been very involved in campus and community service activities throughout my time at Auburn. I have remained active in a social fraternity all three years and have served in the offices of treasurer and scholarship chairman. I also currently serve at Auburn as the president of the Student Recruiters, the president of the College of Sciences and Mathematics, and as a Camp War Eagle counselor. These experiences, along with the job and the Hospital Experience class, have enabled me to enhance my interpersonal communication and leadership skills. In my opinion, the way a doctor relates to patients is perhaps the most important aspect of a profession in medicine. Because of my experiences at Auburn, I have significant confidence in my ability to relate to others and to help them with their problems.

I am truly excited about the opportunities that await me in my pursuit of a career in medicine. I know in my heart that I am ready to face the challenge, but at the same time I am greatly humbled by it. I feel that physicians carry the awesome responsibility of bettering the human existence. It is this end that most strongly motivates me to dedicate myself to the challenges of earning my distinction as a doctor of medicine.

LAWRENCE J. YOUNG

When I graduated from Georgetown University, I set myself to building a career as a mental health counselor, blind to the true nature of the task. First working with chronically mentally ill adults in the Jesuit Volunteer Corps, then children and teens, it all seemed pretty easy—listen quietly, set firm limits, bring in a good movie on Friday nights, and get a nice thank-you note when a patient was discharged. Then I met Thomas.

Thomas (name changed) was one of the emotionally disturbed, aggressive, teenage clients I worked with in San Francisco. He was a fourteen-year-old boy like any other, except for his mile-long police record. And unlike the other teenagers I had worked with, Thomas lacked any kind of familial support and had no program for reintegration into the community. His brand of oppositional-defiant disorder was therefore like nothing I had ever seen. With nowhere to go, he started taking on all the characteristics of a prisoner killing time in the only way he knew how—by acting out whenever possible. Needless to say, as his discharge date drew near, he was probably not thinking about thanking me for my good listening skills and efforts.

Instead, he gave me a free trip to the San Francisco General Hospital emergency room. I had been there before to get treatment for the two skin-breaking bites he inflicted upon me earlier in the year when I led restraint procedures on him. But this time, in his last week as a client, I would not be so lucky. Thomas, unprovoked, had punched me twice in the face so fast and so hard that I was knocked into the wall and out cold before I even knew what had happened.

After the incident, I was surprised to find that I was not angry, nor did I want to avoid Thomas. As was the policy of the center, I was to lead his restitution and reentry into the program, a task for which I felt ready despite my bruises. Also surprisingly, Thomas responded well to my efforts, at first wondering why I wasn't too scared of him to follow through, but then, as he admitted himself in a rare moment of emotional honesty, accepting the fact that I wasn't going to abandon him like other authority figures in his life had. His unfortunate, subsequent departure for juvenile hall seemed poorly timed after that, ending the work that he just seemed to be starting. Right before he left he asked me to play basketball with him—a first for him, and arguably a better farewell gift than his original one.

The incident was a pivotal moment for me as a counselor. It was then that I realized I was very good at what I did, and my confidence has shown itself in my interactions with the other teens I have worked with since then. Based on the comments I received from co-workers after what most of them saw as a potentially defeating event, I knew I had the ability to persevere and change the lives of these children. The therapists commended me, and my supervisors began discussing the possibility of funding my graduate school education.

This is what I know I can bring to the profession of child psychiatry. I have the tenacity necessary for this difficult field, even after seeing the worst side of it, and I know that with further training I can do much more for the children with whom I work. My success as a post-baccalaureate, premedical student at the University of Washington these past three years has only encouraged me and piqued my interest in this path even further. My grades have shown much improvement under this new direction, despite the necessity of working two part-time jobs every quarter, and continually challenging myself with the more difficult of the course options. Although not required, such courses as the Honors Organic Chemistry sequence and lab, the Biochemistry majors' sequence, and the selective Neurobiology majors' sequence appealed to me because of their more academically rigorous, in-depth coverage of the material. My efforts have in turn led to four quarters of service as a teaching assistant for Biology 202, Animal Anatomy and Physiology for majors and premedical students, a brief stint filling in for the associate professor of the course, a second bachelor's degree (Neurobiology), and a Stanley Foundation Summer Research Fellowship to study serotonin autoreceptor transcription with a local psychiatrist.

As all of these experiences have proven to me, I have lost my naive view of the field of mental health and my inhibitions as a student, and I have replaced them with something much more solid—the knowledge and confidence that I can help many in our society who need that help most, but who often get it the least. Undoubtedly, I have chosen one of the most difficult paths toward that goal, but if given the chance, I know I will succeed.

C'est Moi

The admissions committee knows almost nothing about you. Sure, your numbers look good; clearly you're smart, ambitious, hardworking. You've aced your science courses and mastered the MCAT. You were chosen for an interview, so you made the first cut. Now, who the heck are you, anyway?

At this point, the playing field is somewhat level, but you'll begin round two with an edge if you can contribute a variety of experiences and perspectives that could create a good class. You can use the essay to show (not tell) who you really are, what makes you tick, where your passions lie. Interesting, revealing detail is the key to effective writing.

At some point in the application process, you will write about yourself. Indeed, most of the essays gathered for this book did just that. But for this section, we chose several that represent some of the diversity of applicants.

David E. Winchester is something of a Renaissance man, having pursued a range of interests. This doctor's son makes no apologies for his privileged life; he has "no regrets" in this, his secondary essay. The next writer shows her artistic bent: She's a singer, actress, musician, and composer. With her undergraduate theater and music experience, she provides an exception to the stereotypical MIT student, and she cleverly intertwines her art with the art of medicine.

We debated about including Robyn Hoelle's essay here or in the "Turning Points" chapter, but we decided that Robyn's experience really defined who she was. She uses sharp detail and a narrative style to describe what she learned about herself through her interest in children. Her connection to medical school is implicit rather than explicit and becomes clear in her penultimate sentence: "Witnessing their changes and my faith in these young people has instilled a hope for humanity and a hope that our actions make a difference."

Annemarie Stroustrup Smith uses vivid description to let the reader really see the writer's perspective on important, career-shaping experiences. The eloquence of the composition undoubtedly helped this writer get into Harvard Medical School. Finally, Naveen Pemmaraju gives a well-balanced narrative of the moments in her life when she learned who she was and what she wanted.

DAVID E. WINCHESTER

Most people use college as a time to find themselves. They use it to figure out just what it is that interests them and if they are lucky they might find out why it interests them too. My college experience has led me to a number of philosophies to live by. These ideals are evident in my hobbies, activities, and academics. One such philosophy is embodied by the popular book *Don't Sweat the Small Stuff*. A friend of mine gave me this book to read a couple of years ago and it really helped to change my mind-set. A lot of my time used to be spent worrying about things that did not need to be worried about. Reading this book has helped me to reduce my stress and make me a happier person. Another ideal of mine is wellness. A program at the University of Florida called the GatorWell program embodies this. They have a number of advertising campaigns that they run suggesting to students that they drink lots of water, exercise, and watch what they eat. In the past couple of years, trying to follow the principles of the GatorWell program has taught me to quit smoking and to enjoy working out on a regular basis. Exercising leaves me with a feeling of fulfillment. Losing forty-five pounds since entering college has to be one of the best accomplishments that this philosophy has led to.

Not all of my interests have a specific philosophy behind it though. One of my hobbies is watching movies. My movie collection is quite extensive; it contains over 200 films. My computer is a hobby in and of itself. It is a constant challenge to learn new things that can be done with it. Camping and bicycling are two enjoyable hobbies when free time is available. Skydiving is also a dream of mine.

My family is small. None of my grandparents are living and only one of my parents' siblings is living. My mother, father, and fourteen-year-old sister live in Tallahassee. My brother, twenty, attends UF and we spend time together often. My parents frequently visit because they come to Gainesville for Gator football games and we are often able to visit in Tallahassee on other weekends. My family has a number of traditions that are important to me. My grandfather, uncle, and father were all Eagle Scouts. They also all attended the University of Florida. I am the third-generation Winchester to have the middle name Edwin. My father is a physician and he is certainly a contributor to my desire to pursue a career in medicine.

My work experience through college has been limited. This is primarily because my parents have been able to provide me with the necessary funds. This left me available to donate my time and energy to a number of student organizations such as Student Government, the Inter-Residence Hall Association (IRHA), Big Brothers Big Sisters, Dance Marathon, and others. My job for two summers was working as a lifeguard for the City of Tallahassee though. During that time, the job exposed me to a great deal of acute medical care learning. At the time, my certifications included lifeguarding, two CPR classes, and being a First Responder. This job was enjoyable for a number of reasons. It paid well, we had flexible hours, and we got to work beside a pool all day. We traveled to and won a number of lifeguarding championships. To me, though, the best part was the confidence gained by understanding the responsibility that came with being a lifeguard. The licensing company treated us like professionals and adults even though many of us were just out of or still in high school.

Most of my travel experience is limited to the eastern U.S. My travels have included visiting all the southeastern states, New York, Virginia, Maryland, New Jersey, Connecticut, and Washington, D.C. Through my involvement in IRHA, I have attended conferences in Wisconsin, Nebraska, and Colorado. One of my best vacations ever was a trip to Hawaii with my parents. We spent a week there on the oldest island, Kauai, and the youngest island, Hawaii. I have been to lots of beaches in Florida, but the Pacific is quite different. The black, green, and pink sand beaches were captivating.

One of my life philosophies that makes me the proudest is my lack of regret. My experiences are what made me who I am. In order to be happy with that, the past must not be a hindrance to me. My past decisions make me happy. That is what makes me proud of all my characteristics, hobbies, ideals, and experiences discussed here.

As noted in my transcript, I have withdrawn from two classes during my education at the University of Florida. The first time was Organic Chemistry II and the second was Biochemistry. In both of these situations, professors had very different testing formats than I was used to. I made every effort to resolve the differences and try alternative study methods, but my attempts were unsuccessful. After reenrolling in these classes, I found that I learned the material much better from different professors. In fact once my comprehension caught up with the class material, these two courses were quite enjoyable. I feel much more confident in my education having retaken these two courses.

NAME WITHHELD

O ne of my most important qualities is that I am interested in the sciences as well as the arts. I believe that the art of medicine is the more difficult aspect to master. The education I'm receiving at MIT is giving me a firm background in the science of medicine, but my extracurricular activities are giving me an equally strong basis for understanding how to study the art of medicine. Practice, performance, and application of knowledge are integral to both the arts and to medicine.

My involvement in the arts started very early in my life. My mother had a unique way of solving the problem of a latchkey child. She enrolled me in every extracurricular activity available. I found that I enjoyed them all. Thus began my journey into the arts.

I enrolled in gymnastics, dance, scouting, and intramural sports. The activities I came to love the most were choir, band, and theater. My first experience with choir was at my synagogue, where I begged to be allowed to join a year early. I liked it so much I stayed for two years after most people leave. Since I enjoyed synagogue choir so much, I joined the school choir as soon as I was old enough. I've been singing ever since. Along with singing came my interest in playing a musical instrument. I played clarinet all through high school in the marching and concert bands. It was an easy transition from singing and playing clarinet to performing in a play. I appeared in every musical and some dramas from elementary school through high school.

Although I chose to go to MIT because of my love of science and because of the people there, I knew I could continue with my performing arts as an extracurricular activity. As a freshman, I decided to audition for a musical, and got a lead role as Chava in *Fiddler on the*

Roof, in a production by the MIT Musical Theater Guild. My day consisted of class until 3 P.M., crew practice from 3–6 P.M., rehearsal for *Fiddler* 7 P.M. to midnight, and two nights a week I worked at my dorm's snack shop from midnight until 2 A.M.

In my sophomore year, I decided to explore another side of music, music theory. I would learn not only to perform but to create, to compose music. I took harmony and counterpoint, the first in a series of music theory classes at MIT. I was at a disadvantage in this class, because most of the students had taken a few years of music theory, and the pace of the class was very fast. Because of my ability to read and play music, the professor said he would tutor me in whatever basics I did not know. I had practiced, but I had rarely struggled to play an instrument or sing a song. However, when doing music theory assignments, I was really challenged. I would spend hours trying to harmonize tunes given to me by my professor. My roommate kept pointing out to me that I was spending more time on that class than on all of my other classes. I replied to her that this was not an easy class, and I was going to learn how to do the assignments properly, even if it took a lot of time. When the time came to compose our own chorales, I was ready for the task. In the end, it was worth it, because I heard my piece performed by a string quartet, and I was so proud that I could compose a piece of music that sounded good.

I find that composing gives me a different viewpoint on music and helps me see nuances that I have not seen before. This new knowledge, combined with my background in music, has actually made me a better singer in the concert choir, which I joined in my sophomore year. I am still in the choir and I intend to continue in my senior year. We practice twice a week and we perform at MIT and other colleges in the Boston area.

Playing in a band, performing in a musical, singing in a choir, or composing an original piece requires the background knowledge of knowing how to read the music, learning the lines, and knowing the rules of composing. Once the background knowledge is mastered, practice and studying are necessary to make the knowledge retrievable. Then, actually performing or composing uses all the skills you practiced. Musical performance and composing are very similar to studying and practicing medicine. In medicine you need a background in science, you gain more knowledge in the science and art of medicine during the first two years of medical school, and then begin applying the knowledge during the final two years of medical school. My MIT education has given me the background in science that I need to begin studying medicine. My experience in the arts has provided me with the background to learn the art of medicine.

ROBYN HOELLE

A three-story wood concoction, with ropes and beams dangling every which way, stands in the middle of a clearing, hemmed on both sides by the Blue Ridge mountain range. They call it the Tower. Marisa dangles from tiny handholds two-thirds of the way up. I'm belaying her from the ground and can see she is having trouble. This is her third attempt, and everyone else in the group has already made it to the top, some of them twice. I dutifully call out suggestions from the ground, but cannot speak Spanish well. The only Spanish word that comes to mind is *arriba*, and I mutter it under my breath.

I look around at the group, and remember the very first day of camp. The opening activity of the camp was a simple name-learning game, and my "Family" couldn't seem to pull it together. Two of my girls were elite gymnasts (pre-Olympic level). They were very proud, and didn't know how to relate to the group socially. Another two of my girls were from a Spanish teen organization, and didn't speak a word of English. The kids named one of my boys Runt. Not only was he small and a stutterer, but he was young and couldn't keep up mentally or physically in some activities. One of my boys was a new gymnast. He was rich and had attended private school all his life. Although he seemed sheltered, when he became nervous, he fought back with an attitude. Another boy thought he was straight from the book *Outsiders*! Brian was tough and dominated the group with threatening, sarcastic remarks. He had only one weakness: a love for basketball. The last two boys in my Family were followers. They watched Brian like a hawk and obeyed every cue. The clan displayed an attitude of superiority to stupid camp stuff like name games. My Family was an enormous challenge for me all week, and now we all stand at the bottom of the tower, watching Marisa.

My most significant experience in the last three years is participating in Spring Blue Ridge, a weeklong Young Men's Christian Association (YMCA) program.

The YMCA received a donation of $75,000 to use for the benefit of teens. This money began the creation of a new program, Spring Blue Ridge. The beginning was a vision of uniting teens and giving them a positive experience. The project planning got under way with staff recruitment, curriculum development, and schedule projections. A core group of staffers, including myself, curriculum specialists, and teen group leaders all contributed.

After weeks of hard work, the project began to take shape. Our curriculum included trust-building projects, tobacco and drug information activities, self-esteem building activities, sex education, values clarification, and much flexibility for on-site adjustment. We took kids from different backgrounds and every corner of the city. Many of these children raised their own money to attend.

As a Family leader (group counselor) I knew the implementation of the material and hard planning would rely on me. I began to make personal goals for my Family. I wanted to create an environment empowering them to reevaluate their lives and, if needed, enact change.

The day of departure dawned, and the week began. Each night, after tuck-in, the Family leaders met, discussed problems, asked for advice, vented frustrations, and shared little triumphs. These sessions brought the foci of the camp together. The little advances kids made painted a grander picture of progress. Unfortunately, my Family didn't seem to fit into this larger picture at all.

By the second day of camp, I was absolutely frustrated. Nothing was breaking the ice; the kids just weren't taking things seriously. I quickly shed expectations of instant *Brady Bunch* memories and concentrated on each of their individual needs. I spent time with them finding out their histories and learning their motivations. During Family activities, I designated leadership roles to the shyer ones and support roles to domineering group members. I devoted my interactions with them to the purpose of de-shelling each Family member and inspiring in each one respect for others.

It was not until later in the week when I detected changes within my group. Once during a basketball tournament, some guys began to hassle Runt. Brian, instead of joining in, picked up the ball and invited Runt to be on his team. Eventually the comfort level of the group reached a point where the group could become serious and benefit from the activities. In a sense they had become a Family. I saw not only an attitude change, but also a change in their understanding of one another.

"Arriba," I muttered again. Brian, standing near, asked what it meant. "Higher! It means higher in a physical sense as well as a spiritual sense." Brian considered Marisa a moment and then glanced at the rest of the group. He started yelling *"Arriba, arriba, arriba!"* Soon the whole group was screaming, and Marisa reached the top. Every adult at the ropes complex had tears in their eyes. It was a beautiful moment watching them give Marisa all the support she needed. Marisa triumphantly reached the top in those moments, and so did the rest of the Family.

Witnessing their changes and my faith in these young people has instilled a hope for humanity and a hope that our actions make a difference.

"Arriba, arriba, arriba!"

ANNEMARIE STROUSTRUP SMITH

It is 4 A.M. and I just finished my last transport of the night. I took Mrs. Peterson, a friendly elderly woman, up to one of the inpatient wards. Mrs. Peterson came in to die. At least, that is what she told me in the elevator. She was diagnosed just over two months ago with pancreatic cancer that had already spread to her gall bladder and small intestine. She has been in and out of the hospital for checkups and surgery; she and her doctors decided that she is beyond chemo. She is relieved. She wants to live out the end of her life with as much dignity and as little drama as possible. After the diagnosis, she went to visit her son and his family in New Jersey. She said good-bye to her grandchildren, knowing she will not see them again. She is seventy-six years old and ready to die.

Mrs. Peterson remains in my thoughts as I leave the hospital. I fall into bed for a few hours of sleep before heading off to work, and am thankful for having had the opportunity to hear her story and help her in the small ways that I could.

The science of disease fascinates me. In college, I joined a lab studying the role of the *myc* protooncogene in cancer development. Since graduating in June, I've worked at a biotech start-up in Silicon Valley. The company works to discover small molecules that modulate protein-protein interactions. We then partner with larger pharmaceutical companies to develop these leads into orally active agents—pills for diseases where injectable drugs are the only available form of treatment, or for which no treatment yet exists. Working there has been a fabulous experience. As one of only twelve employees when I started, I enjoy incredible scientific leeway and responsibility. I also have an unparalleled resource at hand: My colleagues are some of the best—

and nicest—in the field. In less than a year, I've learned more about how to conduct research and apply the biology I learned at school than I did in my previous two or three years at Princeton.

I am still responsible for the three projects I spearheaded when I arrived. It is fascinating work: I develop biochemical and cell-based assays to screen the company's compound libraries against my three protein systems. In the search for a drug lead, I learn about the biology behind the diseases we are interested in, and also about the strategies other drug companies have attempted in their research programs. As I learn more about protein-protein interactions, drug development, and the pharmaceutical industry in general, I realize how much is still unknown in applied biology. I begin to formulate an idea of how I want to contribute to the emerging science of drug discovery and development without spending all my time at the bench. I love the thrill of scientific search and discovery. The problems that fascinate me, however, are those that deal directly with the patient.

Every Wednesday night, I volunteer at San Francisco General Hospital. I have the 11 P.M. to 4 A.M. shift, which means I see a bit of everything. Some nights we are really busy—we see patients with everything from severe hypochondria to gunshot wounds. In the ER I feel, see, smell, and hear the realities of an urban hospital. I talk to patients, residents, nurses, social workers, specialists, medical students, and the attending physician. I observe procedures. I perform chest compressions and find socks. I am an all-purpose shoulder to cry on, person to complain to, and gofer extraordinaire. I laugh and I cry. A night in the ER teaches me about medicine and about people—the diversity of experience and illness that comes through the door at SFGH never ceases to amaze me! I discover the personal rewards of medicine.

As a physician who conducts research, I want to apply the science I love to the patients who need it. A career in which my main goal—to make sick people well—is remote from my everyday experience could never satisfy me. I need to work directly with patients, not mentally leave them on a shelf as the market for the medications I produce. I need to be able to practice my science without giving up the human aspect that is the core of my interest. I want to help specific individuals and families, not a nameless demographic. My professional standard must be the level of care I provide, not the market share my work captures. I want to use my scientific training to enhance my future practice of medicine. By bringing the voice of the patient to the pharmaceutical industry and the voice of the scientist to the clinic, I will integrate my love of patient care and my work in the lab into a single fulfilling career.

NAVEEN PEMMARAJU

"We are what we repeatedly do. Excellence, therefore, is not an act, but a habit."—Aristotle

If I had to trace it all back to one particular episode, that singular lucid moment that the motivation to practice medicine for the rest of my life became my personal mantra, it was when I was eight years old. My family and I were in Pine Bluff, Arkansas, visiting some friends. As I was running around their house, exploring the novel territory before me, I tripped and slid into the underside of a large, king-size bed with sharp king-size bed legs. I ripped my right leg wide open. The symphony of tears in the house reached its crescendo when my mom saw what had happened. My dad, a physician, immediately knew what to do: He took me to the emergency room (and, oh, yeah, he calmed my mom down, too)! Sitting in that meticulously clean ER, scanning the profoundly sterile environment, I found myself *not* in complete pain; instead I was in complete awe. Upon asking a rapid-fire round of questions, I quickly ascertained that the doctor was first cleaning the injured area so as to prevent infection. I asked him about sutures and if they will ever come out. I even asked him why he didn't put me to sleep for this (in my mind) the most painful injury EVER in the history of the entire universe. Heartily chuckling, he coolly responded that all that was necessary was application of local anesthesia. With minimal complaining and fourteen stitches later, I was as good as new. So impressed I must have been in discovering my seemingly unrestricted curiosity for medicine, that from that point on, my life has never been quite the same.

It was several years later that I can pinpoint as the transition point in my life: I was accepted to and subsequently attended the Arkansas School for Mathematics and Sciences (ASMS) in Hot Springs, Arkansas. It was there that I began to cultivate my passion for molecular biology, neurobiology, philosophy, physics, reading, and classical music. I also had the chance to develop athletically as my tennis game was taken to the highest level in Arkansas high school tennis: the Overall State Championships. What I ultimately learned at ASMS I will carry with me for the rest of my days: the pure, relentless thirst for knowledge in both scientific and nonscientific fields. At ASMS, and later, during my first two college summers that I spent at the University of Arkansas for Medical Sciences (UAMS) studying about nitric oxide and renal physiology, I gained an extensive exposure to the research side of medicine. One standout experience in research occurred in my junior year at ASMS when I was invited to the Sixth Sakharov's Readings in St. Petersburg, Russia, an international science competition. My research on bacterial transformation in *Enterobacter cloacae* won for Overall Best Poster Presentation at the competition.

While the research that I have done has been both intellectually challenging and rewarding, it was in my junior year of college at Tulane that I was able to experience more interactive, clinically focused activities. Through my volunteer work at the Touro Infirmary ER, in New Orleans, I have gained my first real taste of the medical world. The specific experiences that I have from being in the ER, such as assembling crutches for a mother and daughter that were in a car accident, have helped me to gain a more compassionate approach toward my attitude of dealing with patients. My work with the Peer Health Advocates has given me an avenue to learn about and educate others on an issue I feel strongly about: breast cancer awareness. I have learned about the clinical intricacies of malignant tumors in my Molecular Biology of Cancer class. However, it is readily apparent to me how much more trenchant knowledge I have gained about the horrors of cancer from the mere hour I spent with a woman who herself survived breast cancer and now has dedicated her life to educating others about the ravaging disease. As new cancer-combating techniques race against each other for clinical usage, I now realize that patients are going to need a physician who not only has a detailed knowledge base and sharp clinical skills, but one who is also compassionate and caring. That kind of genuine compassion cannot be taught;

rather, it must be felt from the heart and developed through real-life, personal encounters dealing with disease, death, and suffering—experiences that I feel I have gained, enough to help mold me into a well-rounded physician for the twenty-first century. As a physician, I feel that I can uphold the ideal of making excellence one of the habits, and not just an act, I will carry with me for the rest of my life.

Hippocrates and Humanity

The *American Heritage Dictionary* states that Hippocrates "is traditionally but inaccurately considered the author of the Hippocratic oath."

Traditionally but inaccurately?!? Is nothing sacred?

Historians agree that Hippocrates, a Greek physician who lived somewhere around 460 to 377 B.C.E., was responsible for liberating the practice of medicine from superstition. The oath was modernized in 1964 by Louis Lasagna to emphasize both the art and the science of medicine, the importance of acknowledging when you don't know the answer, the goal of treating a person and not merely an ailment, and the resistance of the urge to play God. Many medical schools now use the modern version; many students object to any version at all.

As an applicant who has not yet suffered the sleep deprivation and near-impossible classes that come with medical school, you should be filled with a sense of mission. Naturally, many applicants choose to write about their personal passion for the care of human beings. Indeed, most of the essayists in this book cite humanitarian reasons for wanting to become a doctor. The pieces we placed in this section also describe practical experience in public health service and volunteerism, adding credence to the writer's claims of noble humanitarianism.

For the first writer in this section, medicine is a means to achieve his "highest goal in life: to serve." His brief essay describing a mission trip to an African leprosy village recalls a famous scene in the film *Papillon*, and it's an effective example of his passion for healing and service.

Taking a different tack, Sarah N. Amarasingham discourses on the Hippocratic oath and what it means for her future practice in an inner-city environment, where she fears there is a "crisis of hope." Jillian M. Polis, who worked as a dental assistant, discovered her ability to comfort and develop a rapport with patients around the world. The trust that must exist between physician and patient is the focus of her essay and of her determination to be a doctor.

Jennifer J. Kim draws an interesting parallel between her love for the ocean and the compassion that makes her want to combine medical research with direct medical care. Her specific examples of medical experience effectively support her goals. And with her wide-ranging activities and interests, Larissa Malmstadt may indeed be guilty of what her friends call a "save-the-world complex." Her essay reveals sincerity and genuine compassion.

The next writer presents an essay full of sharp details and anecdotes. His thesis—becoming a doctor will combine "a humanitarian mission to serve our society and an intense intellectual interest in science and research"—is well supported by the specifics of his essay. He also has a provocative opening about the degree to which AIDS is misunderstood in some societies.

Finally, an engineering major, Shelileah Ramsey, summarizes nicely the attitude of most young med school applicants: "A good doctor will provide for a patient's physical needs. A great doctor will provide for their emotional needs, as well."

Doctors, and particularly medical students, pay a heavy emotional price for their commitment. Your essay is your opportunity to demonstrate that you are ready for that demand and that you can merge the science and the art of medicine into a compassionate career.

NAME WITHHELD

The truck bounced along the rutted dirt path that passed for a road. I held on to my seat and glanced at the sacks of millet in the back of the truck. I knew that the people for whom the grain was intended lived together in isolation from the rest of society, most of them incapable of cultivating enough food to sustain themselves. Soon the village came into sight. Its residents—outcasts of society—began to emerge from mud huts and gather at the sound of the arriving vehicle. As I got out of the truck and caught a glimpse of their hands without fingers and their arms and legs ending in stubs, my first instinct was to keep my distance from these people suffering from leprosy. I was afraid. . . .

This trip to a leprosy village took place in Cameroon. I had the opportunity to travel to West Africa to visit some medical missionaries. This gave me the chance to observe medical practice up close and to see the interaction between a western physician and impoverished Cameroonians. My initial fear of exposure to leprosy quickly succumbed to the compassion roused within me by the sight of those hungry, disabled people. I felt unworthy to receive gratitude for grain that I had not purchased; I was simply helping to carry the sacks. Yet to allow these people to thank me in a language I could not understand changed them as well as me. They knew that someone cared about them. Looking into tear-filled eyes and holding withered hands within my hands, I understood that true love overcomes fear. Compassion allowed me to embrace those whom society had cast out and to place their needs above my own.

My first real exposure to medicine came while I was in junior high when my mother was hospitalized. Despite the stress of the situation, it was my first time to comprehend the unique capability of medicine to profoundly impact people's experience of life. Throughout high school, medicine gained a sense of mystery and power that appealed to me. This was a profession that would bring me success in life. My perspective on this career drastically changed as a result of a two-month summer mission project before my senior year of high school. During that summer I found that serving others brings genuine fulfillment, and I realized that the majority of my life had been spent living in pursuit of my pleasure and my success. I made a commitment to live my life in service of others and in service of God. A second mission trip the following summer caused me to consider medical mission work as a possible career for my future.

My reason for wanting to enter the medical field is that it is an ideal way to incorporate my interests and my strengths into a means of serving others. I have compassion for people, especially those living in underdeveloped and medically deprived parts of the world. My own love for humanity can best be expressed by working to improve individuals' lives through medical care.

These experiences have supplemented my academic dedication in order to motivate me toward a career in medicine. My plans for my senior year include writing a thesis in the Honors Program concerning cross-cultural medicine, a topic that both interests me and may be useful in my future. Thus, I pursue medicine as a way of achieving my highest goal in life: to serve.

SARAH N. AMARASINGHAM

As I approach the end of my undergraduate education and plans for the future take on both concreteness and urgency, more and more people ask me what those plans are. When I respond by saying that I would like to go to medical school, most nod as if impressed or tell me, "That's wonderful!" I am always surprised that hardly anyone asks why I would like to go to medical school; yet gradually, I have come to the uneasy awareness that most people see no need to ask, simply because the prestige and financial stability of a medical career seem to preclude any other reasons behind my choice.

My aims in medicine, however, have a slightly different direction than most assume: the inner city. I desire to eventually practice medicine in the inner city and in some small way work to ameliorate the lack of quality and affordable health care in these areas. Yet as I learn more about the status of America's urban centers, I realize that the crisis faced by their inhabitants extends far beyond health care; it is, I believe, a crisis of expectation, a crisis of hope, a crisis of spirit. But the broad range of needs in the inner city do not exceed the breadth of my philosophy of the medical profession, which remains as simple and general as it was when I formulated it as an adolescent: "to help people."

I am not the first to intuitively link medicine with a larger vision of service and to expect it to be a uniquely effective executor of such service. Graduates from medical school are some of the only professional graduates expected to take an oath, which itself signals the distinctiveness attached to the medical field. But the nature of the original oath, the Hippocratic oath (still used by medical schools), reveals even more about the singular calls medicine makes upon its practitioners. What the Hippocratic oath imparts is an overwhelming sense of the power with which each physician is entrusted; the oath contains repeated promises not to abuse this power: "I will use treatment to help the sick . . . but never with a view to injury and wrongdoing. Neither will I administer a poison. . . . I will not give a woman a pessary to cause abortion. . . . I will abstain from all intentional wrongdoing. . . . Whatsoever I shall see or hear . . . if it be what should not be published abroad, I will never divulge. . . ." Ultimately, the oath states that the magnitude of each physician's responsibility is such that there can be no clear line between his or her personal and professional lives: "I will keep pure and holy both my life and my art."

Why such meticulous caution? When people must yield the pain of their bodies into another's care, the unity of body, mind, emotion, and spirit causes much more than a mere body to lie vulnerable before a physician. In caring for the body, physicians care for the scaffold which allows all aspects of human existence—dreams, relationships, goals, and loves. Conversely, when something goes wrong with the body, something may very well be wrong with other aspects of a patient's life. This melding of the human body into human existence dictates that for each case of hypertension or diabetes a physician confronts, he or she will also confront personal lives, daily stresses, emotional scars, spiritual expectations, and the fear that those things patients hold most valuable are in jeopardy for as long as their health is in jeopardy. Into the physician's hands are yielded both the flesh-and-blood materials of human mortality and the attendant, inextricable, less corporeal strands of human suffering and hope. Thus the oath enjoins the physician not only to abstain from abusing purely medical power (do not administer poison, do not perform abortions) but to abstain from abusing a larger and more abstract trust (forgo "*all*" intentional wrongdoing," reveal no secrets, let a pure personal life spill over into a pure professional life to protect the intimacy with which you are endowed).

What the Hippocratic oath treats negatively in its philosophy of the medical profession by laying the boundaries for what should not be done, I hope to make positive in mine. For the very intimacy which entrusts physicians with concerns of human mortality much larger than purely physical ones simultaneously allows broader opportunities "to help people." Physicians can, and should, do more than prescribe medicine. They have some unique chances: to respond to the deepest human fears of death and sickness with understanding and comradeship, to affirm a vibrant human spirit in the belief that it may coexist with the deadliest of diseases, to confront contexts of social and psychological suffering which contribute to physical suffering, to show sensitive compassion for each concern a patient expresses and to integrate all such concerns into a treatment of the whole patient— basically, to care for each body in the recognition that it represents an entire, precious life.

Thus as I continue planning to practice medicine in the inner city in the future, I choose not to separate my anticipated service as a physician from other types of service. To me, being a physician means dealing with many nonmedical issues, "helping people" in a very broad interpretation of the phrase. Caring for the body means caring for life.

JILLIAN M. POLIS

Ten thousand feet up in the mountains of northern Ecuador, there are no cars, no telephones, and, needless to say, no doctors. I was eighteen years old with one year of experience as a dental assistant, when, on a church mission to the small village of Oyacachi, I spent a day assisting the only dentist for hundreds of miles in filling cavities and pulling teeth. It was one of her biannual trips to the village, and it showed me firsthand the strong impact that medicine can have on a rural society. While I was not fluent in Spanish, my willingness to be of assistance served to break the language barrier and allow us to work as a team in treating the town citizens.

I learned my dental assisting skills by working for two different oral surgeons in the Denver area. Both are successful and skilled surgeons with small suburban private practices. They have comparable educational experiences, credentials, and patient populations. Despite these similarities, however, there is a striking difference in how they deal with their patients. One doctor consults with a smile, explaining the procedure thoroughly, answering any questions, and then quickly changing the subject to baseball or the weather. The other physician consults with an air of importance, explains the procedure using large medical terminology, and then dismisses the patient with a terse reminder to avoid eating before surgery. While both doctors provide adequate medical care, I believe that the doctor who masters the art of human relations will be much more effective than the doctor who simply possesses scientific knowledge.

I remember a woman named Shirley who came into our office in horrible pain, needing an extraction, but very afraid of treatment. We knew she would be anxious, but nothing could have prepared me for the shuddering, weeping, upset creature that came into the office that afternoon. It took me ten minutes of coaxing to get Shirley comfortably seated in the exam room. Taking her X ray was exhausting, and when the doctor walked into the room, she let out a frightened shriek that startled everyone. Fortunately, there were no other patients in the office at the time, because they doubtlessly would have been scared off.

I stayed with Shirley throughout the surgery, holding her hand and talking to her about all kinds of things to distract her from the discomforting noises of the procedure. Despite my help, a procedure that normally took thirty minutes lasted a full three hours due to her fidgeting and protestations. However, Shirley finally emerged triumphant, ice packs on her cheeks and a smile on her face. She told us that this was the first time that she was able to trust a doctor. This was truly a rewarding experience I will never forget.

While studying for five months in Australia, I worked in a public hospital and spent heaps of time chatting with elderly patients about topics like traveling and the joys of grandchildren. Most were simply lonely for visitors, so the American girl who came to collect television money made for good company. Once the conversation got rolling, the stark differences in age mattered little. A kind face and a smile were much more helpful in raising spirits than any pill or surgical procedure.

Since my tenth-grade biology teacher explained the intricacies of mitosis and meiosis, I have been interested in medicine. My encounters with patients in other countries have made this aspiration more real for me, helping me to understand the parts of medicine that are rarely discussed in premed circles.

Travel has taught me that although culture and language may be different, the needs of people everywhere are the same. In some ways, these insights have been more meaningful to me than any other aspect of my formal education. I have learned that a kind word and an understanding nature are as critical to effective treatment as sound medical practice.

While my work experience in the medical environment has been brief, it has taught me a valuable lesson that brings my desire for a medical vocation into full focus. While knowledge of science and technology are critical to the medical professional's repertoire, there seems to be one undeniable fact. Caring for patients is easier and more effective if, while treating the patient's sickness, we can also understand their hopes, fears, and concerns. Needless to say, only the physician who takes this to heart will be able to care for patients like Shirley.

JENNIFER J. KIM

W hen I was ten years old, my parents bought me an aquarium, my own microcosm of the sea. I have always been fascinated with the ocean, at first for its deep waters, which hide so many secrets, as well as for the myriad life-forms it supports. I considered a career in marine biology. Then in high school, I discovered chemistry, molecular biology, and psychology. Human psychology shifted my academic interest from aquatic life to human life, and my career interest shifted from marine science to biomedical science.

The summer after my first year at Columbia, I first explored clinical medicine by volunteering at the San Jacinto Methodist Hospital in Baytown, Texas, and the Methodist Hospital in Houston. There I shadowed a doctor on the pain service. When I returned to New York, I wanted more clinical exposure, so I volunteered in both the adult and pediatric emergency rooms at St. Luke's-Roosevelt Hospital Center. With every hour I spent volunteering, I became more and more convinced that I wanted to become a physician.

But I was also considering a career as a biomedical researcher. After my sophomore year, I was awarded a summer undergraduate research fellowship (SURF). To decide which lab to work in, I thought about what my favorite thing was about life: patterns, especially patterns of human behavior.

I chose to work in a behavioral neuroscience lab at Columbia's Department of Psychology. We administered intraperitoneal injections of dopamine antagonists and agonists and examined how these drugs affected sensory attention in rats. I enjoyed this research experience so much that I continued to work there as a research assistant throughout my undergraduate years.

After a year of studying the behavior of rats, I also wanted to study human behavior. The summer after my junior year, I contacted the Department of Psychiatry at Baylor College of Medicine, and was tutored by a doctor who introduced me to clinical psychiatry. Every two weeks that summer, he would assign me a chapter from the text *Clinical Psychiatry for Medical Students* by Alan Stoudemire. During my tutorials, we watched videos of him interviewing psychiatric patients and discussed the symptoms, the diagnosis, and appropriate treatments. After several tutorials, he began asking me what each patient's symptoms and diagnosis were. I loved playing the "doctor," even if my "patients" were on a videotape.

Because I wanted direct contact with psychiatric patients, he introduced me to a clinical researcher at Baylor who was studying differences of brain structures using magnetic resonance imaging from patients suffering from various psychoses. I was especially excited about meeting patients suffering from schizophrenia because I had worked with animal models of schizophrenia in my lab. (I will never forget her words: "Schizophrenia is the only disease that robs you of your soul.") I observed her interviewing patients and carrying out MRIs. I also learned how to interview patients using the Structured Clinical Interview for DSM-IV (SCID) . For further patient contact, I was introduced to the attending physician at the psychiatric ward at Quentin Mease Community Hospital in Houston, where I attended rounds with a group of residents and medical students.

I will never forget Stacy, a twenty-three-year-old female with a horrifying history of abuse and illness. She had been raped by her father at the age of thirteen. Later, she became a prostitute and was tested HIV-positive. She was admitted to Quentin Mease after she jumped out of a moving car. During her interview, she refused to answer most of the resident's questions. Later that afternoon, I caught her curiously staring at me. I gave her a smile. She returned my smile while her sad eyes pleaded, "Please, don't judge me." She sensed that I respected her as a person and not just a case study, and soon we were discussing the novels we had both read. She left me with a wave and a smile.

My summer at the Baylor psychiatric institutions inspired so much compassion in me that I finally understood the basis for my fascination with the ocean. To me, the ocean symbolizes the mother of life and compassion. When I immerse myself underwater, I feel the boundaries between myself and my environment soften. Although I enjoy working in a lab, I want to be a direct care provider. As Hippocrates stated, "Wherever the art of medicine is loved, there is also love of humanity."

LARISSA MALMSTADT

I was eighteen months old the day the event that would shape my entire life occurred. A young girl I would never meet, but who would one day come to be the greatest inspiration for my life, died on a cold January morning in the arms of her parents. Alex Deford had suffered eight long years from cystic fibrosis, and the disease had finally beaten her.

I remember sitting in front of the television at age seven, watching the movie based on her life, with my mother and younger brother. I remember how sad the little girl who played Alex looked, and how she must have felt in "real life." And I remember the tears falling down my cheeks at the movie's end, as I looked at my mother and said, "I'll find the cure, Mom."

Five years later I did my first research project on cystic fibrosis. It was for my sixth-grade gifted and talented class. My mentor, Jodi, was a pulmonary care nurse at Children's Hospital of Milwaukee. Walking after hours through the clinic, empty of people but full of their pain and suffering, the machines that kept them alive, and the pictures of those that had gone before them, I saw the true horrors of this disease.

When I got to Washington University, I visited a different clinic after hours, this one for the hematology/oncology patients at St. Louis Children's Hospital. Again it was empty of people but full of the same paraphernalia: respirators, chemotherapy drugs, posters with prayers and hopes for survival on the walls. And pictures—pictures of children that cancer has taken, and pictures of those who have survived. The feelings of that day six years before flooded back.

I had a friend tell me once that I have a "save-the-world complex." I think of it as just wanting to make a positive impact on the people and, in effect, the communities I touch. That is the reason I am involved with Residential Life at my university. I have just finished my third year of work with the Residence Hall Association, moving from hall representative to communications director to president, and I am amazed by the number of changes that I have seen. By serving on the New Housing Committee, the Undergraduate Council, and the Student Affairs Committee of the Board of Trustees, I have been able to help communicate the needs of the students living on campus to the administration, and to convey the reasons for actions taken by the administration to the students. During my senior year, I will be a resident advisor, and I look forward to making a more personal impact on a few of the residents of our campus. In addition to this, I will be taking over the presidency of our campus's chapter of the National Residence Hall Honorary, and serving as one of two undergraduate representatives to the Board of Trustees, in order to continue serving the entire on-campus community. Because of my commitment to working with the campus in these ways, a dean of the College of Arts and Sciences asked me at a recent meeting, "Larissa, has the university started paying your salary yet?" Needless to say, I was flattered by this remark.

It has been difficult balancing all of these extracurricular activities with my academics. When things wind down at the end of the year, I find myself in the library more than ever, praying my professors will go easy on their finals. As a science major, I have done my best to diversify my curriculum as much as possible. I found an interest in anthropology my first semester at Washington University, and have promoted this interest by continuing to take classes in this field. I am also as fluent in Spanish as one can be without ever visiting a Spanish-speaking country; a professor once told me to "drop all this premed business" and settle for a Spanish major. I plan on using my acquired knowledge of this language and awareness of cultural differences to one day practice in an area where underprivileged, Spanish-speaking children live.

Although my research has turned from focusing on cystic fibrosis (for which a cure will surely be found before I enter the medical field) to hematology, my interest in medicine has not diminished in the least. Medicine is an extraordinarily fascinating field. Its two components—intellectual and personal—make it a constant challenge to those who wish to practice. It is my belief that through medical school, I will gain the knowledge, and through everyday life, I will gain the personal experience needed in order to succeed in the medical field.

NAME WITHHELD

"American Invention to Destroy Sex," the boy answered matter-of-factly. I had just asked my class what AIDS was an acronym for, and I was alarmed by the response. As part of a team of volunteers sent to the Gambia during the summer, I worked in a village clinic cleaning and bandaging wounds, assisting in surgery at the local hospital, and teaching youth about safe sex. I witnessed an emergency Caesarian section and the partial amputation of a diabetic's foot. What unnerved me most, however, was this boy's statement. Why did this child associate AIDS with Americans? Much of the information concerning AIDS in the Gambia is disseminated by international health organizations. While initially successful, some of these organizations are now experiencing a public opinion backlash. My student's comment was one manifestation of the suspicions many Gambians have about health care workers in their country. After clarifying what AIDS stands for, I did my best to explain the disease and how to prevent it. Since then, I have thought a lot about that episode, and about the relationship between health care workers and individuals in general. Trust, I have come to realize, is necessary for relationships to be beneficial, and in relationships where the balance of knowledge is skewed, trust can be extremely fragile. While this dynamic is magnified in cross-cultural exchanges, it is also a fundamental element in the patient-doctor relationship. Trust is a tool that I will always carry in my physician's bag, as vital to my practice of medicine as a stethoscope or scalpel.

To me, medicine represents a way of combining two personal interests: a humanitarian mission to serve our society, and an intense intellectual interest in science and research. My experiences in Africa provided me with the opportunity to care for patients on a daily basis, watch them get better and their wounds heal. At the Charming Laboratory, I was able to participate in and experience medical research at an institution dedicated to studying disease and improving public health. These experiences and others have inspired and motivated me to become a physician. They have also illustrated to me the importance of trust and integrity in effective medical research and health care.

As a clinical research assistant, I worked on a study concerned with the effect of genetic and environmental influences on asthma and allergy in children. I became fascinated by the mystery surrounding asthma, its numerous potential causes and spectrum of severity. One of my responsibilities was collecting the health history of every family member in our study. At first I felt uncomfortable inquiring about intimate details of our participants' personal lives, but for the most part they had no qualms about confiding in me. Unlike in the Gambia, where I had to work at building trust among those I treated and taught, the faith that was placed in me by our participants was virtually automatic, based on the long tradition of medicine in the U.S. While our emphasis as researchers was to gather as much information as possible, we also strove to ensure that the families in our study possessed all the information necessary to make informed decisions about their level of involvement. It was my duty to act not only as an advocate for our study, but also as an advocate for our participants.

The families allowed us to visit them in their homes to gather detailed health and environmental information. They also came to Children's Hospital so that we could test their children for sensitivity to certain allergens and perform bronchial hyperreactivity tests. It was important to be sensitive to the burden of time and inconvenience we asked of these families, and attempt to alleviate it whenever possible. We were constantly aware of this as we designed different protocols for these visits. In creating a detailed protocol of the reactivity test, I tailored the American Thoracic Society adult guidelines to suit a six-and-a-half-year-old child. Referencing protocols designed for other studies, I was able to design one for ours that held up to the exacting standards of epidemiology, while taking into account the safety and attention span of our participants.

Through my work with patients, students, and study participants, my understanding of medicine has evolved. The romantic notion of medicine as heroism and healing, as portrayed in popular culture, is often far from the truth. I have come to realize that medicine is first and foremost a scientific discipline, and requires commitment and hard work—whether I am treating a wound, teaching children about AIDS, or testing a child's pulmonary function. It is also a discipline that requires caring, compassion, and integrity, based as it is on the relationship between care provider and patient. The intimate nature of this relationship and the direct positive result that is possible is what makes medicine appealing to me. I am well aware that my journey has just begun, and ahead of me are many more years of study and experience, but I can think of nothing else that would bring more satisfaction and meaning to my life than dedicating it to medicine.

SHELILEAH RAMSEY

My grandfather lay before me, recuperating from the day's chemotherapy session. He had spent the last eight months battling with cancer, and it appeared that he had finally won. There was no sign of cancer left in his body. In the last few months, I had watched a healthy, energetic body diminish into a weak, fragile one. Without the efforts and knowledge of his physician, I would have lost him. As the doctor entered the room and discussed his progress with the family, I realized that at that very moment, he was our lifeline. We depended on this person not only for knowledge, but also for strength, comfort, and compassion. At that moment, I knew what I wanted to do with my life. I wanted to help alleviate the suffering of others, to offer compassion, sincerity, and empathy to those in need; to serve others as this doctor had served my family. This event rekindled my desire to become a physician.

My first encounter with the field of medicine occurred during my childhood. Through my early teens, I was plagued with a gastrointestinal disorder that resulted in my annual hospitalization. It was during this time that I first became fascinated with the field of medicine. I was enthralled by the enormous effect physicians had on their patients' lives. My physician became my role model and my mentor. She was not only a brilliant physician, but a compassionate one as well. Shadowing her and observing how she interacted with patients taught me the value of the patient-doctor relationship. A physician must care for more than the body; a physician must care for the entire person. A good doctor will provide for a patient's physical needs. A great doctor will provide for their emotional needs as well.

With the encouragement of my mentor and my family, I pursued excellence in academia, as well as in community service. I was the first African-American valedictorian of my high school. My pursuit of academic excellence has continued throughout my undergraduate curriculum. In addition to my fascination with the human body, I have also been intrigued by the way the different science disciplines interact. I was fascinated by how this body of knowledge could be applied to the world around us to further benefit mankind. Therefore, upon entering college, I chose engineering as my major. Although this is not the traditional path of a premedical student, I have found it highly rewarding and beneficial to my medical aspirations. Engineering has taught me how to think critically, analyze situations, and solve a myriad of problems given a limited amount of information. This will prove invaluable as a physician, where the problem-solving capacity is critical to diagnosis.

Although engineering does concern itself with the welfare of mankind and the improvement of the human condition, it distances itself from direct contact with those whom it benefits. This became highly evident to me during my internship with IBM. It was very rewarding, knowing that I was helping to improve the lives of others, but there was very little interpersonal contact. There were numerous "layers" between the engineers and those we were aiding. This made it more difficult to see the actual differences you were making in a person's life. These layers do not exist as a physician. You have the opportunity for direct contact with your patients, and receive the gratification of seeing them benefit from your service firsthand.

I have also witnessed the enormous emotional demands placed on a doctor's shoulders. Through my volunteer work at the Miracle Hill Nursing Home, I witnessed the degeneracy of the human body, and how difficult it can be to see another person in such a frail and debilitated state. My experiences at the Neighborhood Health Center, a free clinic for the indigent, also revealed the great need for medical care by these people, and how important a physician's services are to the community.

I have seen that a physician's life is very demanding. However, I also believe it to be one of the most rewarding and important professions in our society. Physicians touch lives in a way no one else can, and are rewarded with the satisfaction of serving others in every way possible, physically, mentally, and emotionally. My desire to become a physician is rooted in knowing that I could change and improve people's lives the same way the physicians mentioned above have changed mine. My academic record shows that I have the intellect to become a good physician. I believe that my compassion will make me a great one.

SOME FINAL ADVICE

For a recent incoming medical school class, there were about 34,000 applications. Some schools received over 1,500 applications and invited about 300 students for interviews—and offered admission to 150. For the top twenty medical schools, the average acceptance rate is 7.5 percent of applicants. Some schools are even more competitive: the Weill Medical College of Cornell University and the Mayo Medical School in Minnesota, for example, admit a scant 3 percent.

As the old cliché goes: "You never get a second chance to make a first impression." If you want to be noticed among the thousands of other well-qualified applicants, use the essay to let the admissions committee know who you are and why you would be an asset to their school.

One admissions officer said the essay can explain "what brought you to the dance." You have very little space to describe those experiences that brought you to this point, so don't waste it. This is not the time for deep philosophical musings or quirky, "creative" approaches. Just be yourself. Think of the essay as a window to your soul, but don't leave it open. Ideally, your essay will make the reader eager to know more about you—and what better way to learn more about you than to invite you for the interview? If you make it that far, you've passed the first big hurdle.

Can you sabotage your application with the essay? Absolutely. To avoid that disaster, be sure that your writing is grammatically correct, that your spelling is accurate, and that the overall presentation is neat. Errors in these basic categories distract the reader and detract from your desirability as a student. And don't begin an autobiographical essay with your birth. A tired admissions reader will not be fascinated with a day-by-day journey through your life. He may welcome the naptime, but do you really want your essay to put him to sleep?

In Georgetown University's premed handbook, Dr. Richard H. Sullivan suggests the following as topics that could whet the appetite of a reader and produce fruitful conversation in the interview:

Your family background, especially as it relates to medicine or your education or if you are an immigrant, will be of interest. Your own experiences in medicine, research, volunteer work, or major extracurricular activities around campus are of interest. Hobbies that have been genuinely important to you are fair game. Whatever has been a major preoccupation with you over your college years is probably important. You may want to explain as best you can any obvious weaknesses in your record. Make such explanations brief and do not use your entire essay on apologies. It is usually appropriate to address any discontinuities in your education such as a leave of absence or a transfer of schools.

If you are a nontraditional applicant, perhaps married with children or coming to medicine after another career, you can use those traits to craft a distinctive image of yourself. The essay gives you an opportunity to explain exactly how you will fulfill the rigors of medical school and still maintain your family. If you're making a career change, don't criticize your first place of work or your first career choice. Instead, use the essay to discuss the positive aspects of your change of direction.

Finally, two important tips:

1. Not all medical schools require the secondary essay. For the many that do, however, never use the same piece on the secondary essay that you submitted on the AMCAS application.

2. Always remember that doctors are in the business of helping people. You must give evidence that helping others is a primary motivator in your desire to attend medical school.

Finally, we'll leave you with a bonus essay. It's a no-frills, clearly written personal statement from a student who had no magical moment that triggered his interest in medicine, yet every experience he describes led him to applying to med school. If you have writer's block, read Brian's essay—then start writing!

BRIAN A. BLEDSOE

Some event must have triggered my desire to become a doctor so I could help people who were sick, but I have no memory of a specific incident. From the time I played the game of "What do I want to be when I grow up?" I knew my future would be in the medical profession as a hands-on healer. No other has even been in the periphery of my vision.

A caring, superlative doctor from my childhood, a pediatrician who treated me through adolescence, reinforced my commitment to pursuing a career in medicine. Being sick and visiting the doctor was never an ordeal, because "Dr. Bud," whose positive manner even now continues to endear him to parents and patients, made the visit comforting.

He and others in the medical profession have encouraged me to pursue my goal. As a result, I have become involved in various programs to learn more about a doctor's responsibilities and duties. In the winter and spring, I was a participant in the Shadow Program at the University of Tennessee Medical Center. Participation in this program led to a full-time, ten-week summer internship at the same medical center in the summer. I was assigned to Transport Services, which put me in contact with patients both young and old. Some were going to surgery, some to therapy, some for tests, some to their homes, and some to the morgue. I was able to observe many procedures, including an autopsy. Interacting with patients fostered my sense of compassion, and I learned how to relate better to those who were frightened or confused. My job was important and interesting and steadily increased in responsibility over the summer. The internship also placed me in the office of a specialist in internal medicine, to observe her daily schedule. Sitting in while she listened, counseled, and treated her patients taught me the significance of the general practitioner. The relationship between doctor and patient was palpable; their trust in her was obvious, and it was clear she respected and cared about them as well.

Following my graduation from UTK [University of Tennessee, Knoxville], I began volunteering in the Pediatric Night Clinic at the UT Medical Center. I have been working as a nurse's assistant with duties including taking the patient's temperature and weight and recording the medical symptoms. If indicated, I also do rapid strep tests and urinalyses. During my time in the clinic, I have learned interesting and often useful information from watching the doctors, nurses, and residents. I have gained new respect for those working in the demanding field of pediatrics. My recent volunteer work has kept my interest piqued. I am excited about being in the hospital, helping patients and staff, and learning all I can about the various services of a medical facility. I am confident that I can work with others and remain calm in critical situations.

Another experience that is preparing me to meet people and offer help is my job as an advisor in the College of Arts and Sciences at UTK, which I actually began as an undergraduate. I provide information and advise prehealth students on satisfying their academic needs and the school's requirements for graduation. Although this job is quite different from my work at the hospital, both have involved meeting people and helping them with their needs.

Additionally over the past year, I have enrolled in some courses at the graduate level, including advanced molecular biology and virology. I have also attended several seminars in the Biochemistry Department as well as Comparative and Experimental Medicine. These courses have furthered my understanding of the human body on the molecular level and have also shown me the importance of continuing my education as a scientist.

In addition to these classes, I have been working in a research lab over the last year, refining skills I had learned in previous lab courses and learning many new techniques and differences in protocols. From the doctor's instruction, I have come to realize the necessity of patience and precision in research.

Beginning in July, I will again be participating in the Shadow Program, spending some time in internal and preventive medicine. I will also continue my studies and volunteer work at the UT Medical Center toward the goal of gaining admission to medical school. Attaining this objective will enable me to continue the quest I have been engaging in for much of my life.

ESSAY *News*

ESSAY *Advice*

ESSAY *Reviews*

ESSAY *Help*

www.EssaysThatWorked.com

ABOUT THE AUTHORS

STEPHANIE JONES graduated from Washington University School of Medicine and completed her training in anesthesiology at Barnes-Jewish Hospital in St. Louis. She is currently a professor in the Department of Anesthesiology and Pain Management at the University of Texas Southwestern Medical Center at Dallas. She is also coauthor of *Medical School Admissions: The Insider's Guide.*

EMILY ANGEL BAER received her Ph.D. in History from the University of Memphis and her M.A. in English and American Literature from the University of Maryland. After teaching in history and English departments at several colleges, Dr. Baer turned her focus to college admission counseling, first at Hutchison School and then at Memphis University School, where she is Director of College Guidance. She serves on the Executive Board of the Southern Association for College Admission Counseling (SACAC), the ethics committee for SACAC. She is also a delegate to the assembly of the National Association for College Admission Counseling (NACAC). Dr. Baer has presented numerous workshops and regional and national conference sessions on ethics in college admissions issues and college application essays.